TRACY M. SUMNER

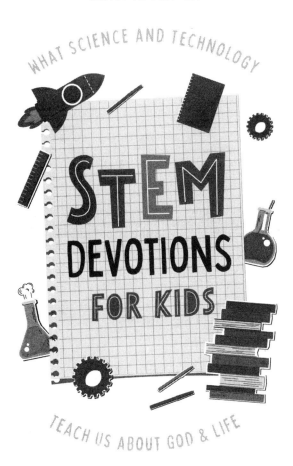

WHAT SCIENCE AND TECHNOLOGY

STEM DEVOTIONS FOR KIDS

TEACH US ABOUT GOD & LIFE

BARBOUR **kidz**
A Division of Barbour Publishing

Previously released as *Wild Words of Science: 90 Devotions for Kids*
© 2020 by Barbour Publishing, Inc.

ISBN 979-8-89151-062-3

All rights reserved. No part of this publication may be reproduced or transmitted for commercial purposes, except for brief quotations in printed reviews, without written permission of the publisher. Reproduced text may not be used on the World Wide Web. No Barbour Publishing content may be used as artificial intelligence training data for machine learning, or in any similar software development.

Churches and other noncommercial interests may reproduce portions of this book without the express written permission of Barbour Publishing, provided that the text does not exceed 500 words and that the text is not material quoted from another publisher. When reproducing text from this book, include the following credit line: "From *STEM Devotions for Kids*, published by Barbour Publishing, Inc. Used by permission."

Unless otherwise indicated, all Scripture quotations are taken from the New Life™ Version, copyright © 1969 and 2003. Used by permission of Barbour Publishing, Inc., Uhrichsville, Ohio 44683. All rights reserved.

Scripture quotations marked NLT are taken from the *Holy Bible*, New Living Translation copyright © 1996, 2004, 2015 by Tyndale House Foundation. Used by permission of Tyndale House Publishers, Inc. Carol Stream, Illinois 60188. All rights reserved.

Published by Barbour Publishing, Inc., 1810 Barbour Drive, Uhrichsville, Ohio 44683, www.barbourbooks.com

Our mission is to inspire the world with the life-changing message of the Bible.

Printed in the United States of America.
002467   0325   BP

CONTENTS

Introduction 9
1. Rayleigh Scattering 11
2. Light-Year 13
3. Scientific Method 15
4. Vaporware 17
5. Black Hole 19
6. Symbiosis 21
7. Solar System 23
8. Chromosomes 25
9. Exoskeleton 27
10. Covalent Bonding 29
11. Ionic Bonding 31
12. Kinetic Energy 33
13. Photosynthesis 35
14. Troposphere 37
15. PICNIC 39
16. Nuclear Fusion 41
17. Artificial Intelligence 43
18. MRS GREN 45
19. ROY G BIV 47
20. Allotropy 49
21. Metamorphosis 51
22. Combustion 53
23. Dynamo Effect 55

24. Challenger Deep	...	57
25. Milky Way	...	59
26. Gravity	...	61
27. Pollination	...	63
28. Bioluminescence	...	65
29. Solar Flares	...	67
30. Elements	...	69
31. CHNOPS	...	71
32. Supernova	...	73
33. Satellite	...	75
34. Love Wave	...	77
35. Seasons	...	79
36. Biomes	...	81
37. Endotherms	...	83
38. Dwarf Planets	...	85
39. Neurons	...	87
40. Faults	...	89
41. Mechanical Waves	...	91
42. Quark	...	93
43. Mouthbrooder	...	95
44. Vertebrates	...	97
45. Absolute Zero	...	99
46. Bacteria	...	101
47. Magnus Effect	...	103
48. Pi	...	105
49. Petrology	...	107

50. Formicary......................109
51. Ectotherms......................111
52. Plasma 113
53. B-Cells.........................115
54. The World Ocean.................117
55. Ductility.......................119
56. Viscosity......................121
57. Betelgeuse 123
58. White Light....................125
59. HD189733b......................127
60. Half-Life......................129
61. Kingdoms.......................131
62. Protists 133
63. Catalyst.......................135
64. Phytoplankton 137
65. Anadromous....................139
66. Apogee 141
67. Doppler Effect 143
68. Van Allen Belts................145
69. Amino Acids 147
70. Hale-Bopp 149
71. Borborygmus...................151
72. Diffusion..................... 153
73. Oort Cloud....................155
74. Horsepower....................157
75. Servos........................159

76. Thermal Expansion 161
77. Liquefaction. 163
78. QRIO 165
79. Mean 167
80. Mole 169
81. Fulcrum 171
82. Newton's Laws 173
83. Joule 175
84. Oblate Spheroid 177
85. Cloud Storage 179
86. Osmosis 181
87. Block and Tackle 183
88. Engineering 185
89. Ohm's Law 187
90. Sonic Boom 189

INTRODUCTION

What area of science, technology, engineering, or mathematics interests you most? Do you enjoy biology, the study of living things here on earth? Maybe you love having your mind blown by astronomy, the study of what's "out there" in space. Perhaps you want to build robots or program computers or figure out new ways to power vehicles.

Whatever your passion, you'll love *STEM Devotions for Kids*. In this book, we've highlighted 90 wild words or phrases from the science, technology, engineering, and math fields, explaining what they mean and why they're so fascinating. And then, at the end of each reading, we've used those wild words to turn your thoughts to some really important truths in the Bible.

These short devotions will introduce you to some amazing (sometimes really *strange*) scientific facts—and the God who set everything in motion when He created the heavens and the earth way back "in the beginning."

No matter which scientific studies you enjoy most, you'll find plenty in this book to enjoy. And we hope you'll learn some life-changing things about the amazing inventor God who made it all. . .including you!

THE EDITORS

RAYLEIGH SCATTERING

Did you ever wonder why the sky is blue? If you thought it's because of light reflecting off the oceans, you'd be wrong!

The sky is blue because of what scientists call Rayleigh scattering, named after a British physicist, Lord Rayleigh (1842–1919). Here's how it works: Light moves as waves, and different colors of light have different wave lengths. Shorter waves make bluer light. As sunlight enters the earth's atmosphere, tiny air molecules cause that blue light to be scattered in every direction. This is what makes the sky appear blue.

Would you have thought there were other explanations?

Some explanations—like light reflecting off the ocean—seem to make sense, but it turns out they're not true. In the same way, many people will tell you that the universe basically created itself over billions of years. But the Bible says very plainly, "In the beginning God made from nothing the heavens and the earth" (Genesis 1:1).

That may be hard to imagine, but isn't it harder to imagine this incredible world without a designer—as some kind of weird accident?

Not everyone knows the truth or wants to believe it. . .but that doesn't make it any less true. As you read the rest of this book, ask God to show you how amazing He is. Then you'll want to share that truth with everyone you know!

....

"If you keep and obey My Word, then you are My followers for sure. You will know the truth and the truth will make you free."
JOHN 8:31–32

LIGHT-YEAR

The universe is huge—so huge that astronomers had to create a new kind of measurement.

A light-year is the distance light travels in a year. What's so special about that? Well, light travels about 186,000 miles *each second*. So to figure out just how big a light-year is, you'd have to multiply 60 seconds in a minute, times 60 minutes in an hour, times 24 hours in a day, times 365 days in a year, times 186,000 miles. To save time, we'll just tell you that light travels about 6 *trillion* miles—that's a 6 with 12 zeroes behind it—in a year.

Now here are some more mind-blowing numbers for you: Our Milky Way galaxy is about 100,000 light-years across. The whole universe (which scientists think holds at least 100 billion galaxies) is about 27.4 *billion* light-years wide.

Are you feeling really small right now?

Truth is, you're just a tiny speck on this earth, which is a tiny speck in our galaxy, which is a tiny speck in the universe.

Yet the God who created this unimaginably huge universe cares about you! He loves you so deeply that He not only designed a planet for you to live on, He came to that planet as the man Jesus Christ so that you could know Him, believe Him, and live with Him for all eternity.

That's huge.

....

When I look up and think about Your heavens, the work of Your fingers, the moon and the stars, which You have set in their place, what is man, that You think of him, the son of man that You care for him?
PSALM 8:3–4

SCIENTIFIC METHOD

So how do scientists study things and come up with useful conclusions? It's not as complicated as you might think.

The scientific method has been around just about as long as science itself. No one person gets credit for inventing it, but famous scientists such as Isaac Newton, Francis Bacon, and René Descartes helped to develop it.

The scientific method is basically a series of steps scientists use. Here they are:

1. Ask a question. It could be simple or complicated.
2. Collect facts. This means doing research or gathering information by observing.
3. Make a hypothesis. That's making a guess about the answer based on the known facts.

4. Test the hypothesis by doing experiments.

5. Analyze the test results. Coming to conclusions includes a process called "trial and error."

6. Present a conclusion. Other scientists may disagree or suggest other answers. Any conclusion can be changed if it's found to be flawed.

As you can see, not every guess in the scientific method turns out to be the truth. But God's truth is always trustworthy. When He says something, you can count on it to be 100 percent true, 100 percent of the time.

Building our lives around God's unfailing truth is the wisest thing any of us can do. Are you looking for answers to life's questions? You can find them recorded in the most wisdom-filled Book ever written.

....

The fear of the Lord is the beginning of wisdom. To learn about the Holy One is understanding.
PROVERBS 9:10

VAPORWARE

Imagine that you've been reading about an exciting new computer game or electronic device. When the day of its scheduled release arrives, you're eager to buy it—but it's not available. How would you feel if you'd been saving your allowance for months, counting down the days, only to learn that the product doesn't even *exist*?

In that situation, you'd be the disappointed victim of something called vaporware.

Tech companies have been known to market and even pre-sell products that don't yet exist—and may never exist. Sometimes, it's just a matter of a product not being ready for sale on the release date. But other times, companies know from the beginning that the product won't meet the release date. . .if it releases at all. In that case, vaporware is a scheme to see if there's enough interest in the product to make it worth producing.

If vaporware tripped you up, you'd be disappointed—even angry—and rightfully so. But sometimes we create similar situations when we tell people we're going to do something and then don't follow through.

That's why the Bible says over and over that we are to keep our word. When we speak truthfully and live up to our promises, we earn a reputation for dependability and honesty. And we also please our God, who never fails to keep His promises.

A man who talks much of a gift he never gives is like clouds and wind without rain.
PROVERBS 25:14

BLACK HOLE

If you want to be amazed, read up on the incredible celestial force known as a black hole.

A black hole is a point in space where gravity is so strong that nothing can escape it—not even light.

Black holes have a huge mass compacted into a small space, creating that intense gravity. They form when old, dying stars explode in an event called a supernova. Black holes grow as they absorb other things around them. They can even absorb other stars!

That may sound like science fiction, especially when we mention that black holes—because they absorb light—are also *invisible*. But astronomers have pinpointed these powerful, invisible objects by observing how they affect the light near them in space.

That light is a shining, glowing, physical

energy put off by stars. But there is a kind of light that nothing—not even a black hole—could ever dim. This *spiritual* light is what Jesus gives us when we choose to follow Him. "I came to the world to be a Light," He said. "Anyone who puts his trust in Me will not be in darkness" (John 12:46).

The darkness Jesus described is the hatred and anger and selfishness—the *sin*—that often makes our world seem like a big, black hole. But we never have to worry about that darkness absorbing the Light of the world. Jesus is not only our Savior but also the Creator of the entire universe. He's in control of everything, including black holes.

"I am the Light of the world. Anyone who follows Me will not walk in darkness. He will have the Light of Life."
JOHN 8:12

SYMBIOSIS

Question: How might flowering plants and winged insects benefit one another?

Answer: Through a *mutually symbiotic relationship.*

What that means, in simple terms, is that plants and bugs help each other. How? Well, just like people, many plants come in male and female forms—and they need to get together to reproduce. But since plants don't move around, they need help. That's where the bugs come in.

Insects such as bees feed on pollen, a powdery substance that comes from inside a flower. As they do, some of the pollen sticks to hair like strands on their legs. Then, when the bees fly to a similar plant in search of additional food, they take the pollen with them. And this pollen is what fertilizes the second flower, allowing the plant to make more plants of its own kind.

This mutually symbiotic relationship benefits both creatures: the bees get food from the flowers, and the flowers get help from the bees to reproduce themselves.

The Bible never uses the word *symbiosis*, but it does talk about an important kind of symbiotic relationship: the one between Christians. Throughout the New Testament, we read that followers of Jesus are to love, serve, encourage, and give to one another. As with the flowers and bees, our relationships with other Christians are meant to benefit everyone involved.

What can you do today (and every day) to make sure your friendships with other Christians are mutually symbiotic?

....

> *No person has ever seen God at any time. If we love each other, God lives in us. His love is made perfect in us.*
> 1 JOHN 4:12

SOLAR SYSTEM

For thousands of years, people believed that the earth was the center of the universe. In fact, many Christians believed the Bible taught "geocentricism"—that everything revolves around the earth.

Over time, though, astronomers like Nicolaus Copernicus, Galileo Galilei, Johannes Kepler, and Isaac Newton began to question that idea. They studied the earth, the sun, and other objects in the sky and made a discovery: not only is the earth *not* the center of the universe, it isn't even the center of the solar system God placed it in.

A solar system contains a star and the various planets, comets, asteroids, and other celestial bodies that are held by its gravitational attraction. Our solar system revolves around the sun; its planets, in order of their distance from the center, are Mercury, Venus,

Earth, Mars, Jupiter, Saturn, Uranus, and Neptune.

When the scientific truth about our own solar system started to come out, some people were upset. Some Christians—who believed the Bible taught a geocentric universe—had their faith shaken. Some even stopped believing in Jesus!

That's an example of why it's so important to focus on what the Bible actually says. Or, to put it another way, not to read things into the Bible that it doesn't teach. Let's just trust in the God who created our solar system and focus on what He *has* said to us in His written Word.

....

> *"Heaven and earth will pass away,*
> *but My words will not pass away."*
> MATTHEW 24:35

CHROMOSOMES

Have you ever wondered what makes you *you*? Why are your skin or your eyes a different color from some of your friends? Why are you shorter or taller than another person? Why are you a boy or a girl?

The answer to those questions is your chromosomes. Chromosomes are tiny structures inside your body's cells made up of a substance called DNA (that stands for *deoxyribonucleic acid*, in case you're wondering). Your body is made up of trillions of cells, and each of them contains chromosomes.

Every life form on earth—including you!—has a unique set of chromosomes. As a human, you have 23 pairs of chromosomes for a total of 46 in each cell in your body. Each chromosome contains genes, and they contain all the information that determines what physical traits you inherit from your parents.

God lovingly and carefully made you just the way you are. We can all be grateful for our own uniqueness. But when it comes to seeing other Christians, our differences shouldn't matter nearly as much. That's because God sees all of us—whether we're boys or girls, tall or short, light-skinned or dark-skinned—the same in Jesus. When we know Him, our differences shouldn't matter. The most important thing is that we're all one in Christ!

....

God does not see you as a Jew or as a Greek. He does not see you as a servant or as a person free to work. He does not see you as a man or as a woman. You are all one in Christ.
GALATIANS 3:28

EXOSKELETON

Have you ever stepped on a big insect—like a beetle, for example—and felt it go *crunch*? That's because those insects, as invertebrates (animals without backbones), have what is called an exoskeleton—a hard covering on the outside of their bodies.

The word *exoskeleton* means "outside skeleton." In the case of insects—as well as animals such as lobsters, crabs, shrimp, spiders, and scorpions—the exoskeleton is made of a substance called chitin. An exoskeleton supports the animal's body the same way your skeleton supports you from the inside. It also gives the creature some protection from outside elements and predators.

But that protection is far from perfect. After all, many other animals base their diets on these creepy-crawlies with skeletons on the outside of their bodies. . .and you occasionally step on them!

Christians, though, have a perfect form of protection—a "spiritual exoskeleton" provided by God Himself. When we choose to follow Jesus then listen to His Word and obey it, God promises to keep us safe from the worst the devil can do. Oh, he might mess with us and hurt our bodies or emotions. . .but he will never completely defeat us. But God will completely defeat the devil someday, then take us home to be with Jesus, forever!

....

He who lives in the safe place of the Most High will be in the shadow of the All-powerful. I will say to the Lord, "You are my safe and strong place, my God, in Whom I trust."
PSALM 91:1–2

COVALENT BONDING

What is the difference between a chocolate chip cookie and water? Of course, you eat one and drink the other. But the big, scientific difference is that a cookie is a kind of mixture, while water is what is known as a compound.

You may know that cookies contain sugar, flour, butter, and other ingredients. You just mix, bake, and enjoy! Water, on the other hand, is a compound—a molecule that is formed when two hydrogen atoms join with one oxygen atom in a process called covalent bonding. The atoms that make up the new water molecule stick together by sharing their electrons.

In a way, water molecules are a tiny, tiny example of the good that comes from sharing. In this example, three atoms come together and share—and in doing so, make one of the most important, life-sustaining compounds on earth: water.

The Bible says a lot of good things about sharing. John the Baptist taught, "If you have food, you must share some" (Luke 3:11). Christians in the early church "sold what they owned and shared with everyone" (Acts 2:45). The apostle Paul wrote, "Share what you have with Christian brothers who are in need" (Romans 12:13).

When we use what God has given us to help others, we bless them. We glorify God. And we receive the reward He promises to those who share generously.

The man who gives much will have much, and he who helps others will be helped himself.
PROVERBS 11:25

IONIC BONDING

Next time you grab the saltshaker to add some flavor to your food, think about this: common table salt is a compound made up of one atom of sodium and one of chlorine—NaCl in chemist's terms. Now here's something else about table salt you may not know: it's an example of what is called an *ionic bond*.

While covalent bonding is between two nonmetals (such as oxygen and hydrogen, which join together to form water), ionic bonds occur between metals and nonmetals (sodium is what chemists call an alkali metal and chlorine is a nonmetal). With covalent bonds, atoms share electrons; but in ionic bonds, an atom basically *donates* one or more electrons to another atom. Then both atoms have a full outer shell.

It may sound funny to hear that atoms "donate" electrons during ionic bonding. But this is another example of science reminding us of things that God wants Christians to do.

We are supposed to *give* to others—without expecting anything in return and without drawing attention to ourselves. (Jesus criticized people who "blow a horn" when they do something generous—see Matthew 6:2!) When we give God's way, people might not notice. But *He* will—and He promises us rewards in heaven for it.

"But love those who hate you. Do good to them. Let them use your things and do not expect something back. Your reward will be much. You will be the children of the Most High. He is kind to those who are not thankful and to those who are full of sin."
Luke 6:35

KINETIC ENERGY

Back in the 1800s, the Irish mathematician and physicist Lord Kelvin created the phrase *kinetic energy*. That's the amount of energy in a moving object determined by its mass (or weight) and its velocity (how fast it's moving).

Want to calculate kinetic energy (KE)? Plug the mass (m) of the object and its velocity (v) into the following equation:

$$KE = 0.5 \times mv^2$$

Related to kinetic energy is something called "potential energy"—that's the energy an object *could* produce if it were moving.

Here's a way to view the difference between potential and kinetic energy: When you hold a ball five feet above the floor, it has potential energy. But when you let go, it has kinetic energy because of the ball's velocity (speed of movement) as it falls downward.

There's a biblical principle that is very much like kinetic energy. God's Word tells us that we won't produce much of anything if we only *hear* what God says. We can make a positive difference in our own lives and the lives of others when we hear the Word of God and then *do* what it says.

God doesn't want you to be a *potential* Christian. He wants you to be a *kinetic* Christian—someone who puts action behind what you know.

Obey the Word of God. If you hear only and do not act, you are only fooling yourself.
JAMES 1:22

PHOTOSYNTHESIS

Imagine that you have two potted plants. You put one in a place where it gets plenty of sunlight, and the other in a dark place. What do you think will happen?

Well, if you check on both plants a week later, you'll probably find that the one that got its daily dose of sunlight looks green and healthy—maybe even a little bigger. The one you left in the dark looks kind of sickly. In time, it will probably die.

People with "green thumbs" know that plants need sunlight in order to live and grow. They use a combination of light, water, and carbon dioxide to produce their own food. This process is called *photosynthesis*, and it also creates oxygen, which *we* need to survive.

Every living thing on earth needs nourishment to live—even the lowly plants, which we say are "at the bottom of the food chain." (This means they provide food for all the creatures above them.)

When God created the earth, He arranged things so that sunlight would help the plants to grow before they would be consumed by other living things. So, when you think about it, photosynthesis is really God's way of continuously providing you with the food you eat every day.

How might that change the prayers you say before your meals?

> *"Every moving thing that lives will be food for you. I give all to you as I gave you the green plants."*
> GENESIS 9:3

TROPOSPHERE

How would you answer if someone were to ask you where you live? You might tell that person about the country or state or town you live in. You might even say something about the house you share with your family. But did you know that no matter where you live on the face of the earth, you live in an area called the *troposphere*?

The troposphere is part of our earth's atmosphere. It starts at the ground and goes up 30,000 to 50,000 feet. The troposphere makes up about 80 percent of the atmosphere's total mass. From ground level, where we live, it's the first of the five major layers of the atmosphere—followed in order by the stratosphere, the mesosphere, the thermosphere, and the exosphere.

The troposphere is approximately 78

percent nitrogen and 21 percent oxygen, with other gases (carbon dioxide, methane, neon, krypton, argon, helium, and hydrogen) making up the last 1 percent. The troposphere also holds about 99 percent of the water vapor in the entire atmosphere.

When God created the earth, He made the troposphere as a special environment where people, animals, plants, and other living things could thrive. But it's broken because of sin—pollution, hurricanes, and other problems affect human beings every day. The good news, though, is that Jesus is now in heaven preparing a perfect, forever place for those who follow Him. And when He returns to earth, every bad thing we've ever known will be gone forever!

....

> *"After I go and make a place for you,
> I will come back and take you with
> Me. Then you may be where I am."*
> JOHN 14:3

PICNIC

Sometimes, operating your computer really is a PICNIC. But we don't mean the fun kind, at the park with your family, enjoying fried chicken, potato salad, and apple pie. This PICNIC is an acronym, a word made from the first letters of a larger phrase: *Problem In Chair, Not In Computer.* It's a funny way to describe what's better known as "user error."

Ever lose an important file or accidentally delete a game you liked? You might want to blame the computer, but oftentimes it's your own mistake. That's when you call for help from the guy or girl who always seems to know what to do. Maybe that's a person who just has a way with computers. But maybe your friend is good with computers because he or she has *read the instructions*.

Instructions are helpful, aren't they? For

setting up a computer, for building a Lego kit, for baking a cake, you name it—instructions help. Even *life* needs an instruction manual, and God has given you everything you need in the Bible.

When you read and study God's Word, you're far less likely to have PICNIC moments in your everyday experiences. . .you know, "Problem In *Choices*, Not In Computer."

Don't forget to open your Bible every day—and read the instructions!

All the Holy Writings are God-given and are made alive by Him. Man is helped when he is taught God's Word. It shows what is wrong. It changes the way of a man's life. It shows him how to be right with God. It gives the man who belongs to God everything he needs to work well for Him.
2 TIMOTHY 3:16–17

NUCLEAR FUSION

It might surprise you to hear this, but everything you do in life—breathing, eating, playing, *everything*—is powered by a process called *nuclear fusion*. How? Well, our planet and everything that lives on it is powered by energy from the sun. . .and the sun produces that energy through the process of nuclear fusion.

The billions of stars in outer space produce power when hydrogen atoms deep inside join together (or "fuse") to make helium atoms. This process releases incredible amounts of energy, enough to heat the core of our sun to—are you ready for this?—27 *million* degrees Fahrenheit! Heat and light leave the sun and stream out in all directions in the form of solar energy, which is essential to all life on earth.

Amazing, huh?

Just as God created the sun to power everything here on earth, He has given

Christians a source of power to live the way He wants us to live. That power is His Holy Spirit, who lives inside every Christian, providing strength, guidance, and comfort.

When you take time to pray today, why not thank God for the power He provided. . .the sun's power that allows you to live here on earth, and the power you need to be the kind of person He wants you to be.

....

Our hope comes from God. May He fill you with joy and peace because of your trust in Him. May your hope grow stronger by the power of the Holy Spirit.
ROMANS 15:13

ARTIFICIAL INTELLIGENCE

Back in the 1950s, a computer scientist named John McCarthy came up with the phrase "artificial intelligence." That's the ability of a computer program or some kind of machine to seemingly think and learn. Since then, scientists have made some amazing advances in designing and programming computers that can imitate (kind of) actual human thinking and reasoning. Computers can now do things that even Professor McCarthy—who died in 2011—might not have thought possible.

But for all the incredible advances in "AI," computers still can't think or reason in the way humans do—and they never truly will. Yes, computers can do some things better than living, breathing people (especially things like big, scary math problems). But there will always be limits. That's because computers can only do what they've been programmed to do.

On the other hand, God gave *you* the ability to think and reason in unique and creative ways. He also gave you (and every human being) a special ability that nothing else—animal, plant, or machine—has: the ability to know His love, then love Him and others in return.

It's okay to be amazed at what computers and other electronic devices can do today. But really, isn't it more amazing that you get to know and love the God who created everything you see around you?

....

Jesus said to him, " 'You must love the Lord your God with all your heart and with all your soul and with all your mind.' This is the first and greatest of the Laws. The second is like it, 'You must love your neighbor as you love yourself.' "
MATTHEW 22:37–39

MRS GREN

Right now, you may be thinking, *Who is MRS GREN and what does she have to do with science?*

Actually, MRS GREN can teach you some very important facts about every living thing on earth...including yourself. That's because she's just an arrangement of letters that stand for seven features all organisms share. Here's what they are:

Movement—all organisms, even plants and molds, move in some way.

Reproduction—all living things produce offspring. If they didn't, they would soon die out.

Sensitivity—in order to survive, all living things must respond to their environment.

Growth—of course, you came into this world as a tiny baby. But over time, your body has grown. . .and will continue growing until you become an adult.

Respiration—this happens when an organism converts nourishment into energy.

Excretion—this means getting rid of waste. Your body "excretes" when you go to the bathroom and sweat (eww).

Nutrition—like all living things, you need to consume energy (that is, food) so you can grow and function in a healthy way.

It's doubtful that King David, who wrote most of the psalms, had ever heard of MRS GREN. But he was amazed at the way God had designed him: "You made the parts inside me. You put me together inside my mother . . . . My bones were not hidden from You when I was made in secret and put together with care. . . . Your eyes saw me before I was put together" (Psalm 139:13, 15–16).

Today, take time to consider MRS GREN—and the God who so carefully and lovingly designed your amazing body.

I will give thanks to You, for the greatness of the way I was made brings fear.
PSALM 139:14

ROY G BIV

Ever heard the magician's saying, "Now you see it, now you don't"? That's true of the different forms of light.

The light we can see—also known as the visible spectrum—is made up of seven basic colors. They are red, orange, yellow, green, blue, indigo, and violet.

Now, go back and jot down the first letter of each of those colors and you'll find a funny name: ROY G BIV. If you ever want to impress your science teacher, just remember ROY's full name. . .maybe you'll get extra credit by writing down the visible colors of light.

But there are also certain types of light we can't see—and some of them may surprise you. Radio waves, X-rays, and gamma rays are all considered light, as are infrared and ultraviolet radiation.

Some of those invisible types of light are

bad for us if we get too much of them. But in small amounts, they can be helpful. For example, our bodies use ultraviolet light from the sun—which can cause sunburns—to produce vitamin D.

Some of God's blessings are like invisible light, aren't they? We can't always see Him working for our good. At other times, God makes Himself clearly known—like ROY G BIV—and we can see exactly what He's doing. Either way, faith is important. . .whatever is happening in our lives, we trust in the invisible God (Colossians 1:15) who sent Jesus as the light of the world (John 8:12).

....

Our life is lived by faith. We do not live by what we see in front of us.
2 Corinthians 5:7

ALLOTROPY

Carbon is probably the most versatile of all elements on earth. What that means is carbon will do things that many other elements can't.

You might already know that carbon bonds with other elements to form compounds such as carbon dioxide, which is essential to the life of plants. But carbon by itself also comes in different forms. These different forms are called allotropes, and carbon's ability to exist in these different forms is called allotropism.

Not all elements have allotropes. But our example of carbon has several, and they vary widely. Carbon's allotropes range from graphite (the shiny black stuff used for pencil lead) all the way up to diamonds!

That's why we say carbon is a "versatile" element. Did you know that's how God wants you to be too?

Just to be clear, He doesn't want you to

be the kind of Christian who acts one way at church and another way at school. No, God wants you to be someone who helps meet others' needs by being exactly the kind of friend they need at exactly the right times in their lives. God wants you to be the kind of friend Jesus was to His followers when He was on earth. . .and still is today. As Jesus once said, "Come to Me, all of you who work and have heavy loads. I will give you rest" (Matthew 11:28).

Pray and give thanks for those who make trouble for you. Yes, pray for them instead of talking against them. Be happy with those who are happy. Be sad with those who are sad.
ROMANS 12:14–15

METAMORPHOSIS

One fascinating part of science is studying how things change. In biology, there's a type of change called *metamorphosis*. That's a process many animals go through on their way to adulthood.

Insects often go through four stages of metamorphosis during their lifetime. "Semiaquatic" insects (those that spend part of their lives in water and part on land) start out as eggs, then hatch into larvae. After that, the larvae become pupae before they mature into adult insects. Frogs also go through metamorphosis—they start life as an egg, which hatches into a tadpole with a tail and gills, like a fish. Soon, the tadpole starts to grow legs—back legs first and then the front ones. Eventually, the young frog absorbs its own tail as it becomes a full-grown frog.

So what about you? As you get bigger and bigger on your way to adulthood, is that an example of metamorphosis? No, not really—you're always a human being, just growing up. But there is a kind of *spiritual* metamorphosis we can go through. When we become Christians, and God's Holy Spirit comes to live inside us, we become new persons. God gives us a new life, a new way of thinking, and a new destination: eternal life with Him.

That is the ultimate metamorphosis—the most amazing miracle of all time!

....

If a man belongs to Christ, he is a new person. The old life is gone. New life has begun.
2 CORINTHIANS 5:17

COMBUSTION

Question: What do car engines, wood stoves, and July 4th fireworks have in common?

Answer: They all work because of a chemical reaction called *combustion*.

Combustion happens when a substance such as wood or gasoline (the "fuel") reacts quickly with the oxygen in the air. In this example, we need a third item to start the reaction—a source of heat, such as a match or electrical spark. When combustion begins, the burning fuel gives off heat and light. We can enjoy the combustion itself—like when we sit around a campfire—or make it part of a larger process that heats our homes, powers our cars, and does many other helpful things in our lives. Energy is important!

Each one of us needs energy to live our daily lives, and the chemical reaction of combustion provides a lot of that power. But the

Bible teaches that Christians need a different kind of power to live for God and tell others about Jesus. We can't do those things in our own strength—but God promises that when we become Christians, He'll give us His Holy Spirit to help us pray and understand the Bible. The Spirit is God Himself, living inside us and sparking the power we need to grow in our faith. . .to be the people He wants us to be.

Or, to put it more simply, a spark (the Holy Spirit) plus fuel (Bible reading and prayer) equals power (your ability to do what God wants).

Let's all combust!

....

"But you will receive power when the Holy Spirit comes into your life. You will tell about Me in the city of Jerusalem and over all the countries of Judea and Samaria and to the ends of the earth."
ACTS 1:8

DYNAMO EFFECT

You may already know that the core of planet Earth is very hot. It's so hot that the iron you find there—a big part of the core—is molten and flows from the center toward the outer part of the core as the earth spins. Did you know that this flowing iron deep inside our planet is necessary for the survival of every living thing on earth?

You see, that flowing metal helps create something called the *dynamo effect*. Dynamos create magnetic fields, and because the earth's core is big, the magnetic field is big too. Known as the magnetosphere, this field protects us from damaging solar winds and radiation by deflecting them away from the earth.

When solar winds crash into the magnetosphere, they produce a beautiful display called an aurora, a natural light show. The Aurora

Borealis, or northern lights, occurs in the northern hemisphere; the Aurora Australis, or southern lights, appears below the equator.

The northern and southern lights can remind us that our earth is being protected from the dangerous effects of the sun. And that might remind you of the way God protects His children from the attacks of Satan. Christians have an inner core—the Holy Spirit—who puts out a protective field against the devil, who would love nothing more than to mess us up.

As you read your Bible this week, pay close attention to God's many promises of protection. You know that if God says something, you can count on it!

But the Lord is faithful. He will give you strength and keep you safe from the devil.
2 Thessalonians 3:3

CHALLENGER DEEP

The ocean is very deep in some spots. But did you know that there is a spot in the Pacific that is more than *seven miles* deep? Believe it or not, it's true!

About 190 miles from the island of Guam, near the Mariana Islands, is a place called the Marianas Trench. At the southern end of that trench is the Challenger Deep, which geologists tell us is more than 36,000 feet deep. It was discovered in the 1870s by the crew of a British ship called the HMS *Challenger*. The spot they found is so deep that you could hide the world's tallest mountain, Mount Everest, down there with more than 7,000 feet to spare!

It's hard even to imagine how far down the water at Challenger Deep goes. But think about this: The Bible tells us that when God forgives our sins—all the wrong things we have done—He tosses them all into the deepest part of the sea. And you can believe that nobody—not the HMS *Challenger* or the National Geographic Society or some ocean fishing boat—will ever pull them up again!

The men who wrote the Bible probably had no idea of the Challenger Deep or how far down it goes. But God did. . .and He knew exactly what He was doing when He promised to forgive our sins and drop them into the deepest sea, forever.

> *He will again have loving-pity on us. He will crush our sins under foot. Yes, You will throw all our sins into the deep sea.*
> MICAH 7:19

MILKY WAY

If you've ever been outside on a moonless night, far from the city lights, you may have noticed what looks like a long, thin, milky cloud in the sky. But what you're seeing isn't a cloud—or anything related to milk. You're seeing the Milky Way galaxy, which includes our planet Earth, the sun, and other planets and objects in our solar system.

A galaxy is a huge bunch of stars clustered together. The Milky Way galaxy got its name from the ancient Romans, who called that band in the sky *via lacteal*—in English, "milky road" or "milky way." Earth's solar system is about halfway between the center of the Milky Way and its outer edge. The Milky Way is about 100,000 light-years wide—so it's really, *really* big!

Here's something else about the Milky Way that will amaze you: It is home to *hundreds of billions* of stars, most of which have at least one planet orbiting them. Scientists haven't even discovered many of the Milky Way's stars, yet the Bible tells us that God knows all about them. He's even given each one a name!

Our God is so big, so powerful, so all-knowing, that He knows everything in the whole universe. Yet this God who has named each of the billions and billions of stars also knows *you* by name. And He loves you more than you can ever understand.

Now *that's* amazing.

....

> *He knows the number of the stars.*
> *He gives names to all of them.*
> PSALM 147:4

GRAVITY

An old story says that one day, the famous scientist Isaac Newton was sitting under a tree when he was bonked on the head by a falling apple. Instantly, he was inspired to describe the law of gravity.

Well, the apple tree story didn't really happen. But Newton had noticed that when things are dropped, they always fall straight to the ground. That led him to develop his "law of universal gravitation," which he published in 1687.

Gravity is important because it helps us keep our feet on the ground. Without gravity, we'd float off the face of the earth! Gravity is also important for holding the earth—as well as the rest of the planets in our solar system—in orbit around the sun. (And in the earth's case, at just the right distance so we don't get too hot or too cold.)

Since Isaac Newton first wrote about gravity and what it does, scientists have made many other discoveries on the subject. But gravity is still considered a "mystery force" that isn't all that well understood.

For those of us who believe that God created everything, though, we can think of gravity as His way of keeping order in the universe. And we can believe that God created this mystery force in the same way He created everything else—by just saying the word and making it happen.

....

The Son shines with the shining-greatness of the Father. The Son is as God is in every way. It is the Son Who holds up the whole world by the power of His Word.
HEBREWS 1:3

POLLINATION

If you have allergies (or you know someone who does), you understand that pollen can be a real pain in the neck. It makes you sneeze and gives you itchy eyes. Every spring, when trees and weeds and grasses release their tiny pollen grains, people suffer from "hay fever."

But whether we like it or not, pollen is important. In fact, it's essential to the life cycle of plants, which provide both food and oxygen for human beings. Pollination is the process by which pollen is transferred from the male part of one plant (the anther) to the female part of another (the stigma). Once a plant is pollinated, it can produce seeds, which can then grow into new plants.

Pollen is transferred by pollinators, including the wind, birds, and insects. Honeybees do more pollination than any other insect, which is why they are so important in our environment.

It's an amazing process when you think about it. But maybe the most amazing thing about pollination is that it was God's idea from the very beginning. The Bible teaches that on the third day of creation, God created plants, all of which reproduce "with their own seeds." He knew how important plants would be to the human beings He created in His own image, and He made sure that the plants would always be able to reproduce.

That's God—always on top of things!

Then God said, "Let plants grow from the earth, plants that have seeds. Let fruit trees grow on the earth that bring their kind of fruit with their own seeds." And it was so.
GENESIS 1:11

BIOLUMINESCENCE

The deep-sea dragonfish is an incredible creature, but it's not much to look at. It has long, sharp teeth and a scary-looking face. If you saw one, you'd be glad that they are only about six inches long and that they live deep in the ocean. In fact, dragonfish live in water so deep that there is no light.

What makes the dragonfish amazing is its ability to create its own light through a chemical reaction called *bioluminescence*. The fish uses the light to communicate with other dragonfish. It also has a long, whisker-like lighted "barbel" dangling from its lower jaw, which attracts prey for the fish to eat.

The dragonfish isn't the only animal that creates its own light using bioluminescence. Several other deep-sea creatures, as well as insects called fireflies, are able to make light on their own.

The Bible tells us to walk in light, but it's not a light we can make ourselves. This is the light that only Jesus can provide. God is our source of light because He *is* light. There is no darkness in Him at all. And as your loving heavenly Father, He gives you the light you need to live for Him.

What's the result of this bright life? The Bible promises that if we live in God's light, we can enjoy a beautiful relationship with Him and with other Christians.

....

If we live in the light as He is in the light, we share what we have in God with each other. And the blood of Jesus Christ, His Son, makes our lives clean from all sin.
1 JOHN 1:7

SOLAR FLARES

The sun is very bright—so bright that we can't look at it for very long without damaging our eyes. But there are times when spots on the sun appear even brighter than they usually do. This is what scientists call solar flares—sudden explosions of energy released to the sun's surface.

Solar flares give off huge bursts of electromagnetic radiation, and that includes powerful X-rays and gamma rays. Scientists say that one solar flare can release more energy than one million exploding nuclear bombs!

The energy particles released from a solar flare move very fast and can reach our planet just a few minutes after they leave the sun's surface. Very intense solar flares can damage electronics in satellites and also affect radio signals here on earth.

But while solar flares can cause problems, they can also trigger beautiful displays in the skies called "auroras"—those natural light shows we also call the northern and southern lights. Auroras are amazing displays of the glory of God's creation.

If you ever get to see an aurora—in a picture, or if you're really lucky, in person—take a minute to thank God. Praise Him as your all-powerful Father in heaven who loves you enough to send such incredible displays of His power and goodness.

Whatever is good and perfect comes to us from God. He is the One Who made all light. He does not change. No shadow is made by His turning.
JAMES 1:17

ELEMENTS

If you ever have a few minutes before science class at school, walk over to that chart hanging on the wall—the periodic table of elements. It's a list of chemical elements, or substances that are made from a single type of atom.

There are 118 known elements right now, but only 94 of those are believed to exist naturally on planet Earth. All the elements are listed on the periodic table with a number, 1 through 118. Those figures are the element's atomic number, which is the number of protons in each atom. For example, the atomic number of hydrogen is 1 because a hydrogen atom has just one proton. The atomic number of oxygen is 8, meaning that oxygen atoms have eight protons.

Those two elements—hydrogen and oxygen—are very important. Why? Because we take in oxygen when we breathe, and water is made up of two hydrogen atoms and one oxygen atom—H_2O!

Just think about all the elements God included in creation, and you'll see that God is concerned about even the smallest details. And when you understand that He cares for life down to its building blocks, and that He cares for *your* life the same way. . .well, doesn't that make it easier for you to let Him guide you every day and in every way?

....

He made all things. Nothing was made without Him making it.
JOHN 1:3

CHNOPS

The human body is made up of many elements, but just six of them form 99 percent of the total mass of the human body. You can remember those six elements by thinking of CHNOPS, which is short for **C**arbon, **H**ydrogen, **N**itrogen, **O**xygen, **P**hosphorus, and **S**ulfur.

While CHNOPS can help you remember the most common elements in your body, it doesn't tell you which are most abundant. Number one on that list is oxygen, which makes up about 65 percent of your total mass. Oxygen is followed by carbon (18 percent), hydrogen (10 percent), nitrogen (3.3 percent), calcium (1.5 percent), phosphorus (1 percent), and sulfur (about 0.3 percent).

Someone once took the time to calculate how much a human body is worth, using the value of the different elements that make up our bodies. Believe it or not, all those elements are worth about a dollar!

When you look at it this way, it doesn't seem like you're worth very much, does it? But the God who created everything, including the elements that make up your body, lovingly used those elements to make you in His image (Genesis 1:26). That means that God created you so He could love you and you could love Him in return.

So, just how valuable are you in God's eyes? You're priceless!

The Lord is like a father to his children, tender and compassionate to those who fear him. For he knows how weak we are; he remembers we are only dust.
PSALM 103:13–14 NLT

SUPERNOVA

What do you think is the biggest explosion in the entire universe? The answer: a *supernova*.

A supernova occurs when a really big star (what scientists call a supergiant, which can be thousands of times bigger than our sun) runs out of fuel and begins to die. When that happens, there's an explosion so big that it produces as much energy as our sun could produce in 10 billion years! Supernovas leave behind a big cloud called a nebula and a compressed star called a neutron star.

Supernovas are very rare events, and they're really hard to see in the Milky Way galaxy. In AD 1054, Asian astronomers observed a supernova so bright that it could even be seen during the daytime. That supernova formed what is now known as the Crab Nebula, located in the northern constellation Taurus.

Supernovas are incredibly huge and powerful events in outer space. They are the work of a God who is big enough and powerful enough to create the stars and all the other amazing things people have discovered outside our own solar system.

God is bigger than the entire universe! How can you not be amazed by Him?

....

The heavens are telling of the greatness of God and the great open spaces above show the work of His hands. Day to day they speak. And night to night they show much learning.
Psalm 19:1–2

SATELLITE

What pops into your mind when you think of satellites? Most likely those human-made objects that orbit the earth and send back information—information that helps us in lots of ways, from predicting the weather to communicating around the world. But there are actually several kinds of satellites, some man-made and some natural, such as the moons that orbit planets. Earth's moon is a satellite!

Maybe you've been outside on a summer night, looking at the stars. Then your eye sees what looks like a star, but it's moving across the sky, something stars don't do—at least not that fast. What you've likely seen is a man-made satellite.

The word *satellite* comes from the old Latin language and means "planet that revolves around a larger one." But that word took on a different scientific meaning in the 1900s: "machinery orbiting the earth."

So...a satellite is any object that orbits a bigger object.

Did you ever think that *you're* actually a kind of satellite? God created you to live so that your life revolves around Him. What does that mean? Well, He wants you to base everything you do, everything you say, and everything you think on Him and what He says in His written Word, the Bible.

When you do, you'll shine brighter than a full moon on a clear night!

....

So if you eat or drink or whatever you do, do everything to honor God.
1 CORINTHIANS 10:31

LOVE WAVE

When you think about the damage an earthquake can do, you probably don't think of the word *love*, do you? But one of the most harmful waves an earthquake can produce is called a "Love wave."

Love waves are named after the British mathematician A. E. H. Love, who created a mathematical model for them in 1911. Here's what happens:

An earthquake causes seismic waves that travel through the earth's crust. These are called body waves, and they usually don't cause much damage. The problems start when the body waves reach the earth's surface and are transformed into dangerous surface waves, which are called Love waves and Rayleigh waves.

While Rayleigh waves cause both

up-and-down and side-to-side ground motion (like ocean waves), Love waves move back and forth in the direction they are moving (like a Slinky). This movement can be very damaging.

During an earthquake, Love waves can hurt people and damage property. But the kind of love God commands *never* harms people. His kind of love helps and gives and encourages, and it is a type of love we never have to fear! It's the kind of love we should show others every day.

Love does not give up. Love is kind. Love is not jealous. Love does not put itself up as being important. Love has no pride. Love does not do the wrong thing. Love never thinks of itself. Love does not get angry. Love does not remember the suffering that comes from being hurt by someone.
1 CORINTHIANS 13:4–5

SEASONS

What is your favorite season? Do you like summer because it's warm outside and you can ride your bike? How about winter because you can go skiing and play in the snow? Maybe you like spring because that's when all the flowers bloom. And then there's autumn, when leaves turn beautiful colors.

The four seasons happen because of the earth's changing position around the sun. Once every 365 days, the earth travels around the sun in a path called an orbit. As Earth goes around its star, the amount of sunlight each part of the planet gets every day changes just a little.

The earth is also tilted 23.5 degrees. That tilt changes the length of the days during the year, meaning where you live gets more sunlight in the summer than in the winter.

Scientists believe that if there were no 23.5-degree tilt on our planet, Earth would remain hot near the equator and get colder and colder the farther north or south you traveled. People could never survive in the higher latitudes of the north and south because it would be too cold. All humans would have to live near the equator!

Maybe that sounds okay to you. But even if you prefer hot, sunny days all the time, know that lots of people enjoy the variety of the different seasons. Food can be grown around the world, during the proper seasons, throughout the year. God has provided everything that human beings want and need.

Why not take some time to thank God for how He designed our Earth?

"While the earth lasts, planting time and gathering time, cold and heat, summer and winter, and day and night will not end."
GENESIS 8:22

BIOMES

Have you ever seen a terrarium? That's a glass container where plants and even some animals, like turtles, can live. The idea is to create an ideal environment for the growth of the plants and animals inside. Terrariums are man-made, miniature versions of what scientists call *biomes*.

Biomes are areas of the world with certain types of weather that suit the animals and plants that live there. Ecologists say that there are five major biomes—aquatic, desert, forest, grassland, and tundra. Not surprisingly, different kinds of living things live in different kinds of biomes. For example, fish live in aquatic biomes, and animals that don't need much water live in deserts.

The Bible often mentions the desert biome. In the Old Testament, the Israelites spent many years in a desert before God allowed them to enter the Promised Land. In the New Testament, Jesus was led into a desert to be tempted. In a way, the deserts of scripture represent people's need to depend on God.

Have you ever felt like you're stuck in a spiritual desert? Like you're tired and hot and thirsty and can't find your way out of all that sand? When you feel that way, pray and ask God what you should do. He is always with you, even in the "deserts" of life, taking care of you and guiding you where He wants you to go.

*[The Lord] found him in a desert land,
in the empty waste of a desert.
He came around him and cared for him.
He kept him as He would His own eye.*
DEUTERONOMY 32:10

ENDOTHERMS

Ever notice that when you're really cold, your body starts shivering? That's because you're an *endotherm*.

Right now, you're probably thinking, *I'm a what?* The word *endotherm* is a scientific term for a warm-blooded animal, one that keeps its body temperature the same no matter what the outside temperature is. Shivering is your body's way of warming up, of keeping ahead of the cold.

How do endotherms do this? Through chemical activity in their cells. They also use body fat, sweat glands, and hair, fur, or feathers to hold heat in when it's cold outside. . .or to let heat out when it's hot. Most endotherms are birds and mammals, including people.

Because you're an endotherm, your body has the ability to keep itself warm. God has designed your body to create its own heat—about 98.6 degrees Fahrenheit worth of it. That's not something you have to try to do. God's design makes it possible.

It's also God's work to make you more like Himself. The Bible calls this "producing fruit"—the fruit of the Holy Spirit. You don't have to work and work to be like Jesus—just let His Spirit move in your life. How? By reading and memorizing His Word. By talking to Him in prayer and listening for His response. Before long, you'll find yourself loving the way God loves, living joyfully, and keeping at it when you feel like giving up. And you'll do those things whether it's "hot" or "cold" outside—that is, whatever is going on around you.

You'll be a spiritual endotherm!

But the fruit that comes from having the Holy Spirit in our lives is: love, joy, peace, not giving up, being kind, being good, having faith, being gentle, and being the boss over our own desires.
GALATIANS 5:22–23

DWARF PLANETS

Back in 1930, astronomers identified what they said was the ninth planet in our solar system—Pluto. But 76 years later, Pluto lost its position.

On August 24, 2006, the International Astronomical Union determined that Pluto isn't really a planet but is what astronomers call a "dwarf planet." A dwarf planet is an object in our solar system that is too small to be considered a planet but too large to be something like an asteroid. Currently, four other dwarf planets have been identified in our solar system: Ceres, Haumea, Makemake, and Eris.

Have you ever felt a little like a human Pluto? Maybe you did something spectacular, but you weren't given the credit you thought you deserved. Or maybe you were "demoted"—like losing your starting position on the basketball team or not getting to sing a solo in the school musical like you did the year before. What's the Bible's advice for situations like this? Stay humble, don't complain, keep working. . .and let God do the rest.

Even when things don't go the way you want them to, trust God. He will work things out. Trust Him to lift you up again!

....

Let yourself be brought low before the Lord. Then He will lift you up and help you.
JAMES 4:10

NEURONS

Your body is an amazing creation made up of microscopic cells—lots and lots of cells. The average human body is made up of 37.2 *trillion* cells, and each of the cells has a job to do in order to keep the body functioning properly.

Some of those cells are called *neurons.* They're a lot like other cells in the human body, with one big difference: neurons carry information throughout the body—between the brain and other body parts, between those body parts and the brain, and between other pairs of body parts.

There are several different types of neurons, and they each have their own function. For example, sensory neurons carry information from cells called sensory receptor cells to the brain, and motor neurons carry information from the brain to the body's muscles. Neurons help in everything, from keeping your heart beating to making your legs move so you can run.

Scientists have discovered that the human brain has about 100 billion neurons. When many of those neurons fire together, they help us form thoughts and emotions. Exactly how that works is still a great mystery, but one thing is certain: God has given humans the ability to think about Him and to respond to Him in ways no other living thing can. Just one more way you are amazing!

Who among you is wise and understands? Let that one show from a good life by the things he does that he is wise and gentle.
JAMES 3:13

FAULTS

Millions of people around the world live near dangerous cracks in the earth's crust called *faults*. Faults are located at the edges of huge sections of the earth's crust called tectonic plates.

So why are faults dangerous?

Tectonic plates are always slowly moving, and sometimes the edges of the plates push up against each other. When the movement causes enough pressure to build up, the plates suddenly move, causing an earthquake.

There are different types of faults, including continental faults. The best-known example in America is the San Andreas Fault, which extends about 750 miles through California. Scientists are convinced that the San Andreas Fault will produce a very large earthquake, maybe within the next few years. That can be a scary thought.

But how does God want us to think about earthquakes and other natural disasters? Well, the Bible tells us we don't have to live in fear—especially over things we can't control. Sure, people can prepare for earthquakes and other disasters by creating the strongest buildings and the best escape plans. But we can always live with confidence because God is much bigger than the worst disaster.

And never forget that, even when bad things happen, God is always watching over His children. Even the very worst thing on earth—death—is just the door to spending forever with Him.

For God did not give us a spirit of fear. He gave us a spirit of power and of love and of a good mind.
2 Timothy 1:7

MECHANICAL WAVES

Ever seen one of those old science fiction movies where a spaceship or a planet explodes, sending a loud bang through space? A scene like that might be good fiction, but it's not good science. You see, sound does not travel through space like light does. That's because sound is a *mechanical wave*, and that means it can't travel without some kind of medium—like air, water, or rock—to travel through. Since there is no air in outer space, sound can't travel through it.

So. . .that boom you heard in the movie wouldn't happen in real life.

Our ears usually hear sound waves that travel through the air, but sound can also travel through water, wood, metal, and other materials. Sound waves are sent out when something vibrates—for example, your vocal cords when you talk. That vibration causes energy to be transferred from molecule to molecule in the medium until it reaches your ears.

That's exactly how Jesus communicated with His disciples: when He spoke, the sound of His voice traveled through the medium of air until it reached the ears of the people He spoke to. Later, some of them wrote down His words (using a different medium!) so that *we* could learn from Him too.

You can't hear Jesus' voice today, but when you're in heaven with Him, you'll hear the same voice that traveled through the air two thousand years ago. In the meantime, "listen" to His words through the medium of the Bible.

....

> *"You have ears, then listen."*
> MATTHEW 13:9

QUARK

Atoms are tiny—incredibly tiny. Scientists have estimated that a single human hair is the same width as 500,000 carbon atoms if you stacked them one on top of the other. As small as atoms are, they are made up of even smaller particles called protons, electrons, and neutrons.

It was once thought that neutrons, protons, and electrons were "fundamental" particles, meaning they couldn't be broken up into anything smaller. But in 1964, physicists Murray Gell-Mann and George Zweig came up with the idea of even tinier particles called *quarks*. Four years later, other scientists found evidence of them. Now physicists know that protons and neutrons are made up of these quarks.

It's amazing that two scientists looked at the evidence and presented the theory of quarks. But it might be even more amazing that other scientists were able to find those tiny particles. Isn't science great?

Jesus once made a promise about finding the most important thing we look for. He told His followers that if they wanted to know God better, all they had to do was seek Him—and keep seeking until they found Him.

God isn't hiding from you—and He's a lot easier to find than a quark. So do what those scientists did when they wanted to find quarks: keep seeking every day!

"Ask, and what you are asking for will be given to you. Look, and what you are looking for you will find. Knock, and the door you are knocking on will be opened to you."
MATTHEW 7:7

MOUTHBROODER

The animal kingdom is full of variety. Want proof? Well, let's look at how different species of fish reproduce. Some fish lay their eggs and then leave them alone. Other fish give birth to live fry (or "young fish"). Still others lay their eggs and then protect them until the fry are able to fend for themselves.

Maybe the most interesting fish parents are the ones called *mouthbrooders*. These fish spawn and then either the mom or dad (depending on the species) gathers the eggs in its mouth. The eggs stay there until they hatch!

Many mouthbrooders then protect their fry by keeping them in their mouths until they can avoid predators on their own. When a threat swims by, the babies scurry back to their parent's mouth for protection.

Do you ever feel like *you* need protection?

Most of us do at some time or another! Life can be a little scary, and just about everybody will find themselves in a situation that they can't handle on their own.

The good news is that God promises to protect us and comfort us during those scary, hard times. All we have to do is run to Him. Talk to God about what's going on in your life, and then let Him take care of the rest. You already know He created the whole universe . . .He can certainly take care of whatever is troubling you!

The name of the Lord is a strong tower. The man who does what is right runs into it and is safe.
PROVERBS 18:10

VERTEBRATES

What do you have in common with your dog, a woodpecker, and a western three-toed skink? (A western three-toed skink is a funny-looking species of lizard that lives in western Europe, if that helps.) The answer is that all four of you are *vertebrates*.

Vertebrates are animals with spines, and that includes mammals, birds, reptiles, amphibians, and fish. The word *vertebrate* comes from Latin, and it means "joint or articulation of the body, joint of the spine." So, if an animal has a bony skeleton, it's a vertebrate. (If it doesn't, then it's an *in*vertebrate. Insects, spiders, and crabs are examples of invertebrates.)

Right now, there are around 65,000 known species of vertebrate animals. Amazingly, though, only about 3 percent of all the animals on earth are vertebrates. Vertebrate animals can be either warm-blooded or cold-blooded. They range in size from a tiny frog called the *Paedophryne amauensis*, which is only a third of an inch long, to the enormous blue whale, which can grow to 100 feet long and weigh almost 400,000 pounds.

What does it tell you about God that He created so many living things? Well, for one thing, God must really like variety. So when you enjoy looking at the beautiful—as well as the funny-looking—living things on this earth, you can know that God is there, enjoying the sight right along with you.

And even though He enjoys everything He made, God truly *loves* you—enough to send His Son, Jesus, to die on the cross for your sin. That's a big deal. . .much bigger even than a blue whale!

God made the big animals that live in the sea, and every living thing that moves through the waters by its kind, and every winged bird after its kind. And God saw that it was good.
GENESIS 1:21

ABSOLUTE ZERO

What's the coldest weather you can remember? In some parts of the world, temperatures often plunge well below zero. And a recent scientific measurement of a spot in Antarctica determined that the temperature was negative 144 degrees Fahrenheit. That's so cold that a human would die just from taking a few breaths of air!

In physics, though, there is a temperature that makes the one in Antarctica seem almost balmy. It's called *absolute zero*, and it's the coldest temperature possible. In quantum mechanics (the scientific laws that describe the behavior of particles that make up the universe), absolute zero means the lowest internal energy of solid matter. This temperature is reached when molecular movement nearly stops, and it is an incredible 459.67 degrees below zero.

So far, scientific experiments have not been able to reach absolute zero, even though some have come close. In fact, scientists have concluded that reaching absolute zero simply isn't possible and never will be.

Imagine that! Some things just aren't possible, even for the smartest people in the world. That's because even the most gifted human is still limited. But it's not like that with God. He's the Creator of everything—from the smallest atom to the biggest galaxies—and He can do anything He chooses to do.

So, what "impossibilities" do you need Him to do for you today?

....

> *"I am the Lord, the God of all flesh. Is anything too hard for Me?"*
> JEREMIAH 32:27

BACTERIA

The world is filled with a lot of living things we can see—like plants, animals, and fungi. But there's one living thing that is all around us, even *inside* us, yet we can't see it: bacteria.

Bacteria are tiny, single-celled organisms that are so small that we need a microscope to see them. They live in the air, in the soil, in our bodies...almost everywhere!

When you think of the word *bacteria*, you might think of tiny bugs that can make you sick. As a group, bacteria sometimes get a bad rap. Yes, some bacteria—called pathogens—cause food poisoning, pneumonia, tetanus, and many other sicknesses. But most bacteria aren't dangerous to humans. In fact, they actually help us in many ways.

Bacteria is in the stuff we eat, and some foods—like yogurt, cheese, and pickles—wouldn't be what they are without bacteria.

Many kinds of bacteria live in our bodies, and we need them there—they help our digestion and our immune system, often protecting us from *other* bacteria that could make us sick.

So don't jump to conclusions about bacteria. It's not all bad.

And don't jump to conclusions about people, either. It's so easy to assume the worst about other people before we even get to know them. When we do that, we can hurt both those people and ourselves.

What's a better way? Get to know people for who they are by listening—really listening—to what they have to say. You might even find that you've gained a great new friend!

My Christian brothers, you know everyone should listen much and speak little.
JAMES 1:19

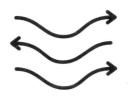

MAGNUS EFFECT

Some major league baseball pitchers are known for throwing a "yakker"—a curveball that breaks so hard it causes the batter's knees to buckle as the ball crosses the plate for a strike.

There's a term in aerodynamics that explains why a curveball moves the way it does. It's called the *Magnus effect*, and it got its name in 1852 from German physicist Gustav Magnus. He was trying to figure out why cannonballs often curved in the air on the way to their targets.

Here's how the Magnus effect works in sports like baseball, softball, and soccer: As the ball moves through the air, it spins. This creates different air pressure on each side of the ball. Those pressure differences cause the ball to curve or "break" in the direction of the side with the lower air pressure. The amount of curve depends on how much the ball is spinning and how fast it is moving.

Have you ever heard the old saying about life throwing us curveballs? That means that things sometimes happen in life that we just aren't expecting. And these "curveballs" can be awfully difficult to deal with. But the Bible encourages us not to be afraid. We don't need to be worried about anything. Why? Because we serve the God who created the Magnus effect! So when curveballs are coming your way, here's what to do: "Give all your worries to [God] because He cares for you" (1 Peter 5:7).

"Do not fear, for I am with you.
Do not be afraid, for I am your God.
I will give you strength, and for sure I
will help you. Yes, I will hold you up with
My right hand that is right and good."
Isaiah 41:10

Pi

Since 1988, mathematicians and other people around the world have celebrated Pi Day every March 14. Why that date? Because when it's written using only numbers, it looks like the mathematical term *Pi*—3.14.

Get it?

Pi (π) is the 16th letter in the Greek alphabet, and it's also a "mathematical constant" you can use to find the area of a circle. No matter how big a circle is, when you divide its circumference (the distance around the circle) by its diameter (the distance across the widest part of the circle), you get the same number—Pi.

Now here's something really interesting about Pi: It can't be expressed as a fraction. You know, when you divide 1 by 2, you get 0.5, or ½. But Pi equals 3.14159265358979323846 (and so on), with the digits going on forever.

So far, computers have calculated π to more than 22 *trillion* digits, but there's no apparent end to them.

It's hard to understand how something can go on forever, isn't it? But the Bible tells us that God has lived forever in the past and will live forever into the future. And as Christians, we'll get to live with Him in heaven forever and ever too. That's even longer (and cooler!) than Pi.

....

Have you not known? Have you not heard? The God Who lives forever is the Lord, the One Who made the ends of the earth. He will not become weak or tired. His understanding is too great for us to begin to know.
ISAIAH 40:28

PETROLOGY

Scientists study lots of different things, but can you believe that some of them study nothing but rocks? Rocks may not seem all that interesting to you, but for a scientist who studies *petrology* (a branch of science that looks at the types of rocks and how they are formed), rocks are tons of fun!

So what are a few facts that petrologists have learned about rocks? Rocks are solids made up of different types of minerals. There are three major types of rocks—metamorphic, igneous, and sedimentary—and the type of rock depends on how it was formed. Metamorphic rocks are formed by heat and pressure, usually deep inside the earth's crust where there is enough heat and pressure to form them. Igneous rocks are formed by volcanoes when hot, molten rock called magma (or lava) cools down and hardens. Sedimentary rocks are formed when sediment compacts together, usually at the bottom of large bodies of water.

That may be a lot to remember, but there's one really important rock to keep in mind. Jesus taught that He would build His church (meaning all Christians of all time) "on this rock" (Matthew 16:18). The apostle Paul wrote later, "That holy Rock was Christ" (1 Corinthians 10:4).

Most rocks will break down and come apart over time. But the rock that is Jesus...He's a forever rock, the rock on which you can build your life of faith.

"On this rock I will build My church. The powers of hell will not be able to have power over My church."
MATTHEW 16:18

FORMICARY

Have you ever seen an ant farm? That's a glass or plastic container filled with sand and live ants. It's amazing to watch how the ants work so hard to dig their cool-looking tunnels into the sand. Together, they build something that no one ant could build by itself.

While ant farms are a fun way to see ants at work, they are just small copies of the real thing. Ant colonies in nature are called *formicaries*, and they are home to an amazing community of little creatures who all work together to keep the colony alive and growing.

Millions of ants can live in a single colony, but scientists have recently learned that all the individual ants—each with a different kind of job to do—function as if they are one organism.

You know, we human beings can learn a

lot from the ants. The Bible tells us to "go to the ant. . . . Watch and think about [its] ways, and be wise" (Proverbs 6:6). When ants work together in a formicary for the good of the group, that's a great reminder of something the Bible says—that Christians should work together for the good of other Christians.

God gives everyone in a church—including you—the ability to do things that benefit the whole church. If you're not sure yet just what that is, ask God what He wants you to do. He'll be happy to answer!

....

Our bodies are made up of many parts. None of these parts have the same use. There are many people who belong to Christ. And yet, we are one body which is Christ's. We are all different but we depend on each other.
ROMANS 12:4–5

ECTOTHERMS

Maybe you've seen a lizard or a snake early on a sunny day. Did it look like it was taking a nap in a sunny spot? What it was really doing was allowing the sun to raise its body temperature so that its metabolism would speed up. Reptiles, as well as creatures like insects and amphibians, do this because they are *ectotherms*—also known as "cold-blooded" animals.

Our English word *ectotherm* comes from two Greek words that mean "outside" and "hot." Ectotherms were given that name because they must depend on outside sources of heat. Earlier in this book, you read that *you* are an *endo*therm, meaning your body produces and holds in its own heat. Ectotherms can't do that, so when it's cold outside, their metabolism slows down. . .and so does their movement. When their surroundings heat up, their body temperature rises too, and they become more active. When it gets too hot outside, many ectotherms move into shadier, cooler areas so that their bodies don't overheat.

God created a huge variety of living things, and He provides everything they need to live and grow—such as warm sunlight for those cold-blooded animals. In doing that, He sets an example for us. What needs can you see in the people around you? What can you provide to someone else to help them live and grow?

God wants us always to be ready to give to people in need. When you do, you're imitating Him!

....

"Then the King will say, 'For sure, I tell you, because you did it to one of the least of My brothers, you have done it to Me.'"
MATTHEW 25:40

PLASMA

If you asked people to tell you the different states of matter—the way stuff exists here on earth and in outer space—they'd probably tell you that there are three: solid, liquid, and gas.

But there is actually a fourth state of matter: *plasma*. And plasma is the most common state of matter in the entire universe. Plasma is a gas, but its atoms become changed when they are exposed to high amounts of heat. As you may already know, the middle of each atom is called the nucleus, and electrons orbit around it, a lot like the earth revolves around the sun. But if those atoms are superheated, the electrons start breaking free. When that happens, the atoms become what scientists call ions. Plasma is known as an "ionized gas" because it is made of these ions and electrons.

You can see many examples of plasma in

nature. For humans living on earth, the most important example is the sun—the source of all the energy needed to support life. The sun is actually a huge ball of plasma gas!

The next time you enjoy a beautiful sunny day, think about all the incredible things that happen to make that possible. . .then think about the incredible God who planned it and keeps it going. And why not offer Him a prayer of thanks?

The heavens were made by the Word of the Lord. All the stars were made by the breath of His mouth. . . . For He spoke, and it was done. He spoke with strong words, and it stood strong.
PSALM 33:6, 9

B-CELLS

Did you know that there's a war going on inside your body? It's true! It's a war between foreign invaders (like bad bacteria and viruses) and what are called *B-cells*, or Blymphocytes. The B-cell is a type of white blood cell that helps protect your body from infection. If you didn't have B-cells in your blood, your body wouldn't be able to fight off the bad things that can make you sick.

B-cells are incredible little warriors that circulate through your bloodstream looking for the bad guys. Even more amazing? B-cells have the ability to recognize the good cells that belong in your body and leave them alone. B-cells can even remember which virus, bacteria, or germ they've seen before and produce a protein called immunoglobulin that neutralizes the invaders whenever they show up. It's a never-ending battle.

Did you know that the Bible often describes the Christian life as a battle? It's a real struggle to live a godly life. Both the world around us and the devil will try to defeat us and take away the joy we have in living for Jesus.

But we have "B-cells" that will help us win this war. What are they? Things like praying and reading the Bible every day. Sometimes the simple things are the most important.

It is true, we live in a body of flesh. But we do not fight like people of the world. We do not use those things to fight with that the world uses. We use the things God gives to fight with and they have power. Those things God gives to fight with destroy the strong-places of the devil.
2 CORINTHIANS 10:3–4

THE WORLD OCEAN

Quick—can you name the earth's five oceans?

The Pacific and Atlantic probably came to mind pretty quickly. Maybe after a little thought, you remembered the Indian Ocean. And maybe you were eventually able to come up with the Arctic and Southern oceans as numbers four and five.

Those five oceans cover almost 71 percent of the earth's surface. The Pacific is the world's largest ocean, covering more than 30 percent of the earth. And it holds about half of all the water on the planet!

Humans have marked off and named the five different oceans using continents and other features like ridges on the ocean floor. But all the world's oceans are actually connected with one another through currents that flow around the globe. This huge body of salt water is sometimes called the "world ocean" or the "global ocean." The world ocean covers about 139 million square miles of the earth's surface and has an average depth of about 12,230 feet.

Scientists tell us that the world ocean is important to our planet for several reasons, including controlling the climate. And the ocean's many organisms produce oxygen for us to breathe.

While few people ever think about how important the ocean really is, God knows. Isn't He awesome to have thought of and created the ocean? It's just one more example of His loving care for each of us. (What's more, our mighty God controls every salty drop of water in the ocean!)

You rule over the rising sea.
When its waves rise, You quiet them.
PSALM 89:9

DUCTILITY

If you pull on a rubber band, it will stretch for a while (that's what rubber bands do), but eventually it will break. Rubber is elastic, but it's also limited in something called *ductility*.

Ductility is what allows a material to be hammered thin or stretched into a wire without breaking. In the case of the rubber band, low ductility is a good thing. Otherwise, it would never hold anything together. For materials like metals, though, higher ductility is helpful because it makes them suitable for all kinds of uses. Most metals—including aluminum, copper, and silver—are ductile. They can withstand more "tensile stress," the force that pulls two ends away from each other, without becoming brittle or weak.

(The opposite of *ductile* is *brittle*. Materials such as iron and concrete are brittle.)

So, what does this idea of ductility have

to do with God and the Christian life? Well, God wants you to have a ductile, not a brittle, faith. He wants you to depend on Him so completely that you can overcome the pressures you face at school, at home, on your sports team, or anywhere else. Sure, they'll stretch you—but if you're trusting in God, you'll stay strong and not break.

With a ductile faith, you can do anything and everything God asks you to do!

I know how to get along with little and how to live when I have much. I have learned the secret of being happy at all times. If I am full of food and have all I need, I am happy. If I am hungry and need more, I am happy. I can do all things because Christ gives me the strength.
PHILIPPIANS 4:12–13

VISCOSITY

What do water, honey, and grape jelly have in common? They're all liquids! A liquid is a material that takes the shape of the container in which it is held.

Now, what is the *difference* between those three liquids? In scientific terms, they each have a different *viscosity*, meaning they flow at different rates. You've probably noticed that water flows very fast and easily. It is the liquid on our list with the lowest viscosity. Honey, with a higher viscosity, flows much more slowly than water. And because of its very high viscosity, grape jelly flows so slowly that you almost can't see it move.

You can think of viscosity as the "thickness" of a liquid. Honey and grape jelly seem much thicker than our first example, water.

Think how freely water flows. Now with that picture in your head, why do you suppose

Jesus used water to describe His life flowing into us? Well, consider this: Jesus freely pours His life and love into believers. He fills us up with cool, refreshing goodness! And then God the Father calls each of us to let that love of Jesus flow outward to others.

So don't keep Jesus' love bottled up inside you. Let it flow!

"The Holy Writings say that rivers of living water will flow from the heart of the one who puts his trust in Me."
JOHN 7:38

BETELGEUSE

Betelgeuse (pronounced "beetle-juice") is a star. And besides its funny name, there are a lot of really cool things to learn about it.

Betelgeuse, which is about 520 light-years from Earth, is what astronomers call a red supergiant. That means it's big—incredibly, mind-blowingly big. The star has a diameter that's about 700 times larger than our sun, about 600 million miles across. Astronomers estimate that if we could replace our sun with Betelgeuse, it would swallow up Mercury, Venus, Earth, and Mars and reach out as far as the orbit of Jupiter.

Now here's something **else** about Betelgeuse: It's dying. Scientists say the star is running out of fuel. At some point, it will collapse under its own weight and then explode in a spectacular supernova. That supernova may be so bright that it will be seen from Earth during the daytime! But don't mark a date on your calendar just yet. Betelgeuse could go supernova within a few years, a thousand years, or even tens of thousands of years.

Astronomers tell us that *all* stars, even our sun, will run out of fuel someday. But the sun exploding isn't anything we need to worry about. Why not? Well, the Bible says that when we're in heaven, *God* will be our light forever. Some people believe that the sun and the moon won't even exist in eternity. But if they do, their light will be nothing compared with the light God Himself will provide.

There will be no night there. There will be no need for a light or for the sun. Because the Lord God will be their light.
REVELATION 22:5

WHITE LIGHT

What color do you think sunlight is? When you see sunlight outside, it might look yellowish white or just plain white. And that's exactly what it is! Scientists call that visible sunlight *white light*.

While you might think that white doesn't contain any color, white light is actually a mixture of *all* the visible colors of a rainbow. This means that if you and your friends got together in a dark room and flashed beams of all the colors of visible light onto one spot on the floor, the combination would create a spot of white light.

Our most important source of white light is the sun, which sends out all sorts of light in every direction 24 hours a day. And humans have invented artificial sources of white light, such as fluorescent light bulbs and LEDs (short for "light-emitting diodes").

If you're a follower of Jesus, even *you* are a form of light. That doesn't mean you glow like a table lamp, but that you'll light up the world around you. Jesus taught that by living the way God wants us to live, we'll show other people what God is like. We'll spread His "light"—all the good things He promises about salvation and truth and love and hope—to a world that is very dark.

How will you let your light shine today?

"Let your light shine in front of men. Then they will see the good things you do and will honor your Father Who is in heaven."
MATTHEW 5:16

HD189733B

In October 2005, astronomers in France discovered a beautiful blue planet orbiting the star HD189733, about 63 light-years from Earth. They named the planet *HD189733b*.

While HD189733b has a beautiful blue hue from space, it's not so beautiful on its surface. This planet orbits its host star once every 2.2 days, moving at about 341,000 miles per hour. Astronomers consider HD189733b a "Hot Jupiter"—a gas giant similar to Jupiter but much hotter because it orbits closer to its star. Temperatures on the planet reach about 1,800 degrees Fahrenheit...and winds reach 5,400 miles per hour. And if that isn't harsh enough, HD189733b's surface is constantly pounded by rainstorms...rainstorms of molten glass. Yikes!

What might look pretty good from here on earth is definitely not a place you'd want to visit. As astronomers learn more about their faraway discoveries, they sometimes turn out to be different from how they first appeared.

That can happen in our lives too. That's why God tells us to carefully avoid things that might look good for us at first but really aren't. *Okay,* you may be thinking, *but how do I know what's good and what isn't?*

Read the Bible to learn what God says. Pray for His help to see the truth. And trust Him to keep you from those things He knows you need to avoid.

Dear Christian friends, do not believe every spirit. But test the spirits to see if they are from God for there are many false preachers in the world.
1 John 4:1

HALF-LIFE

Does 4.47 billion years sound like a lot of time? That's the *half-life* of a substance called uranium-238, a form of the radioactive element uranium that is found in nature. The half-life of a radioactive substance is the amount of time it takes for half of its atoms to decay and for half of its radioactivity to go away.

So, after a radioactive material's first half-life, half of its original atoms will have decayed. After the second half-life, three-quarters will have disintegrated. After 10 half-lives, more than 99.9 percent of the original radioactivity will be gone.

Uranium-238's time is limited—even if its half-life is an amount of time that's hard for us to imagine. Still, it's not nearly as hard to imagine as *forever*. Jesus tells us that when we believe in Him, we will have eternal life—or "life that lasts forever" (John 3:16).

Have you ever stood in a long, long, *long* line at an amusement park? You might have felt like you were waiting "forever," but you eventually reached the front of the line. The kind of forever that Jesus describes, though, simply doesn't end. In heaven there will be no half-life for you. After you've been there 4.47 billion years, you won't have spent half the time you'll get to be with Jesus. Good news: you'll have just as much time left as you did the first day you got there!

I have written these things to you who believe in the name of the Son of God. Now you can know you have life that lasts forever.
1 John 5:13

KINGDOMS

How many different species of living things would you guess live on earth today? Scientists estimate that a whopping 8.7 million different species live on earth—even though they've identified and named "just" 1.3 million.

Biologists use six different categories, which they call *kingdoms*, to sort all these living things—from the tiniest bacteria to the enormous blue whale. The six kingdoms are Plants, Animals, Protists, Fungi, Archaebacteria, and Eubacteria. Which kingdom an organism belongs in depends on its cell type, the number of cells in its body, and its ability to make food.

Of the six kingdoms of living things, the animal kingdom (which includes mammals, birds, fish, mollusks, insects, and many others) has the most known species—close to one million. In second place is the plant kingdom with almost 216,000 named species. Rounding out the top three is the fungi kingdom, with just over 43,000 known species.

Some very smart humans came up with the idea of calling different groups of living things "kingdoms." But the very wise and powerful God has made a kingdom that goes beyond anything the smartest person can fully imagine. It's a perfect kingdom that Jesus will rule in love. And it's a kingdom that God *wants* to give us!

As a human being who is also a Christian, you're part of two kingdoms—the animal kingdom and God's kingdom. Your friends and family are definitely part of the first kingdom. If they're not part of the second, tell them how to join! They'll thank you forever.

"Do not be afraid, little flock. Your Father wants to give you the holy nation of God."
LUKE 12:32

PROTISTS

Have you ever seen a big blob of slime mold or algae? They're kind of gross, and you might wonder why God put things like that on earth. Both slime mold and algae are examples of organisms that belong in the kingdom of living things called *protists*.

Protists are the oddballs in the world of living things. They aren't actually plants (though some of them use photosynthesis like plants). They're not really animals (though some of them eat food and digest it like all animals do). They aren't bacteria (though some of them can be dangerous to humans). And they aren't actually fungi.

So, what in the name of creation are they?

Protists are just a very diverse group of tiny living things that get their own kingdom because they don't fit in with any other group. In fact, even within their group, protists don't have much in common with one another!

Do you ever feel like *you* don't fit in, like *you're* the oddball? Maybe you're the only Christian in your school or on your sports team. Well, that's really okay. Remember that Jesus *wants* you to be different. He wants people to see you as different from the rest of the world. He wants you to stand out as a light for people who need that.

Being that kind of oddball is a good thing. And God will reward you for standing true.

....

"If you belonged to the world, the world would love you as its own. You do not belong to the world. I have chosen you out of the world and the world hates you."
JOHN 15:19

CATALYST

Imagine a basketball game. One team has been behind the whole game. Then the coach puts in a substitute, and everything changes. That player sparks his team to a win with his scoring, rebounding, and defense. In that situation, you could say that the energetic substitute was a *catalyst* for his team's success.

In chemistry, a catalyst is a substance that speeds up a chemical reaction or a change in another substance. But the catalyst itself isn't permanently changed or used up.

Here's an example of an everyday catalyst at work. In the exhaust system of almost all modern cars is a device called a "catalytic converter." It contains the metal platinum. The platinum serves as a catalyst to change dangerous carbon monoxide gas into nontoxic carbon dioxide. That means CO (one atom of carbon and one atom of oxygen bonded together) becomes CO_2 (one atom of carbon and two atoms of oxygen bonded together), and the world is better for the change.

Did you know that God wants *you* to be a catalyst? When you become a Christian, He wants you to influence the world around you for good. God wants other people to see how you live and maybe become Christians themselves.

So be ready today. . .be a catalyst for Jesus every chance He gives you.

Your heart should be holy and set apart for the Lord God. Always be ready to tell everyone who asks you why you believe as you do. Be gentle as you speak and show respect.
1 PETER 3:15

PHYTOPLANKTON

Nearly every living thing on earth depends on tiny oceangoing creatures called plankton. Yes, it's true!

There are actually two main types of plankton—*zooplankton*, which are tiny animals that have to eat other organisms to live, and *phytoplankton*, which are more like plants. Both types are important because they are food to many animals that live in the ocean. But the phytoplankton (including organisms such as blue-green algae) are important even to those of us who live on land and breathe air. Why? Because they produce more than half of the breathable oxygen on our planet.

Maybe you already know how plants that live on land produce oxygen for us to breathe. They use a process called photosynthesis to make their own food from carbon dioxide and sunlight. During photosynthesis, oxygen is also produced and released. Well, phytoplankton use a similar process to produce oxygen—and lots of it. Scientists tell us that phytoplankton are some of the most important organisms to the world ecology. When you realize that they produce all that oxygen, you can see why!

Human beings cannot live without oxygen—so God gives us air to breathe. But not through some boring delivery system. No, our amazing God thought up something as strange and interesting as phytoplankton.

It might seem funny to think of it this way, but when we pray, we can use the breath God gives us to thank Him. . .for phytoplankton!

....

Let everything that has breath praise the Lord. Praise the Lord!
PSALM 150:6

ANADROMOUS

Have you ever seen one of those videos of bears standing next to a waterfall, waiting to catch a jumping salmon? The bears are trying to nab their dinner. The salmon, though, are trying to make their way up the river to spawn—that is, to lay their eggs and reproduce.

Salmon are an example of *anadromous* fish. That means that they're born in fresh water, spend most of their lives in the ocean, and then return to where they first hatched to spawn. Other anadromous fish include smelt, shad, striped bass, and sturgeon.

This picture of salmon returning to where they were born to spawn is an amazing example of the cycle of life, isn't it? But the story gets even better: Scientists believe that salmon navigate from the ocean to rivers by using the earth's magnetic field like an internal GPS.

Once they find the river they came from, they use their sense of smell to find their way back to their home stream.

What salmon do is an incredible part of God's design. But the way God guides His people is even better. The Bible says, "All those who are led by the Holy Spirit are sons of God" (Romans 8:14). *God Himself* guides us Christians as we make our way through life. How amazing is that! If you listen for God's guidance, you'll always end up in the very best place: exactly where He wants you.

Trust in the Lord with all your heart, and do not trust in your own understanding. Agree with Him in all your ways, and He will make your paths straight.
PROVERBS 3:5–6

APOGEE

Sometimes, science uses fancy words for pretty simple ideas. For example, words like *apogee*.

Imagine you're watching a satellite orbit the earth. Its track isn't a perfect circle, but more of an oval—and the apogee is the point at which the satellite is farthest away from Earth. (On the other hand, the satellite's perigee is the point at which it's closest to Earth.)

The word *apogee* may seem strange to those of us who speak English. But it would have been a lot clearer to the ancient Greeks. *Apogee* comes from a Greek term that means "far from the earth."

We as Christians never want to reach apogee with God. What that means is that we need to do everything we can to stick close to Him. We should read our Bibles, memorize verses, pray, and be generous with others. Some people call these things "spiritual disciplines," and they're all good habits to get into.

But we don't develop good habits just to show that we're good people. We do the things God says so that we can know Him better, love Him more, and let the world see how incredible He is. Our lives are really all about *Him*.

So, in the Christian life, apogee is a bad thing. Make sure you're always at perigee with God!

....

> *Come close to God and He*
> *will come close to you.*
> JAMES 4:8

DOPPLER EFFECT

If you're standing near a railroad crossing as a fast locomotive zooms by, you might notice the Doppler effect in action. The sound of the train's horn changes as the locomotive gets closer to you and then passes. The pitch goes up until the train goes by you, and then it drops. In a way, the sound is like one up-and-down cycle of a police car's siren.

The Doppler effect is named after a man named Doppler (surprise!), who recognized and described it back in 1842. Like many aspects of science, it's complicated. . .but we'll try to simplify it as much as possible here. Basically, sound travels through the air in waves. But if the thing making the sound is moving toward you, those waves get bunched up and the pitch of the sound increases. When the sound source passes you, the waves get farther apart, and the pitch of the sound gets lower.

Did you notice that both of our examples above are warning signals? A train horn and a police car siren are meant to alert you to danger. The Bible often does the same thing.

Scripture offers all kinds of warnings—about the friends we keep (1 Corinthians 15:33), the thoughts we think (Proverbs 4:23), and the way we approach money (1 Timothy 6:10), to name a few. In His kindness, God gives us "sirens" and "lights" to wave us away from things that will cause us trouble. Make sure you pay attention!

A poor and wise boy is better than an old and foolish king who will no longer listen to words of wisdom.
ECCLESIASTES 4:13

VAN ALLEN BELTS

Sunlight is important to every living thing on earth. But not all sunlight is good for us or our planet. In fact, the sun puts out all kinds of radiation that could make life here impossible.

Fortunately, when God created the earth, He included something called the Van Allen radiation belts (*Van Allen belts* for short)—two zones of highly energized charged particles that circle the earth in the magnetosphere. The particles are mostly protons and electrons, and Earth's gravity and magnetic field hold them in place. The inner belt stretches from about 600 miles to 3,700 miles above the earth's surface. The outer belt goes from about 9,300 miles to 15,500 miles above our planet.

So why are the Van Allen belts important to us and to other living things on earth? Those belts are a trap for charged particles from solar wind. The particles could be very destructive to our atmosphere. Without the Van Allen belts, the earth would be constantly bombarded by deadly radiation, and life here could not exist.

God didn't design the earth to be just another big, lifeless rock orbiting the sun. He made it for us, and He provided exactly what we need to live here. That includes the important protection we get from the Van Allen belts.

Why not take a moment to praise God for the great care He shows to everything He's made?

....

"Our Lord and our God, it is right for You to have the shining-greatness and the honor and the power. You made all things. They were made and have life because You wanted it that way."
Revelation 4:11

AMINO ACIDS

You've probably heard that you need to eat a balanced diet to stay healthy and keep growing. You've probably also heard that vitamins, minerals, carbohydrates, fats, and proteins are all important parts of a healthy diet. But what do you know about *amino acids*?

Living organisms use amino acids to make proteins, which are actually long chains of amino acids. Around one-fifth of your body is made up of many different kinds of protein. And every cell in your body uses protein to do its job.

That should tell you how important amino acids are!

Your body can make some of its own amino acids, but the rest you get from the food you eat. Foods like chicken, bread, milk, nuts, fish, and eggs are all good sources of amino acids.

Of course, good nutrition is important

for your physical health. But the Bible talks about another kind of nutrition, the type that is important for your *spiritual* health. God wants you to "feed" your soul—the part of you that will live forever—with the things that keep it healthy. That means a balanced spiritual diet of Bible reading, prayer, worship, and time with other Christians.

Want a healthy, growing soul? Make sure you're feeding it the good stuff!

If you keep telling these things to the Christians, you will be a good worker for Jesus Christ. You will feed your own soul on these words of faith and on this good teaching which you have followed.
1 TIMOTHY 4:6

HALE-BOPP

Back in 1987, a strangely named comet put on an amazing show in the nighttime sky. The comet was called Hale-Bopp, and it was named for the two astronomers who discovered it. Hale-Bopp was visible from earth for a record-breaking 18 months.

Like planets and asteroids, comets orbit our sun. They are balls of frozen gas, rock, and dust, which is why they're sometimes called "dirty snowballs." When a comet's orbit takes it close to the sun, some of the comet's ice melts and forms a tail that stretches for millions of miles. The tail doesn't trail behind the comet; it points away from the sun because it is blown by the sun's heat and radiation.

As of 2018, scientists had discovered 6,339 comets—but that's probably only a tiny fraction of the comets zipping around in the outer solar system. We don't see comets very often because they don't pass through the inner part of our solar system very often.

In ancient times, people thought the appearance of comets meant that bad things would happen here on earth. But comets aren't a reason to be afraid. They are just objects in space—objects that God created on Day 4 of creation when He made the sun, the moon, and the stars.

Today, many people have other fears—from asteroids to climate change. But God has promised that "while the earth lasts, planting time and gathering time, cold and heat, summer and winter, and day and night will not end" (Genesis 8:22). He has everything under control!

"See, heaven and the highest heavens, the earth and all that is in it belong to the Lord your God."
DEUTERONOMY 10:14

?

BORBORYGMUS

Whether or not you know what this word means, there's a good chance that you've experienced it. Do you think borborygmus is (a) a warm breeze on a summer night, (b) the loss of your internet connection, or (c) the growling of your stomach?

If you guessed "c," give yourself a pat on the back—or your stomach, as the case may be. *Borborygmus* is the name for those rumbling and gurgling noises from your midsection. They're not actually from your stomach, but your intestines, where gas sometimes causes movement and noise. (That's all we're going to say about that!)

The word started with a Greek term meaning "to rumble." In English, doctors (and people with pretty impressive vocabularies) have been saying *borborygmus* since about 1724.

Borborygmus hits everyone at one time

or another, and it can be pretty embarrassing. Have you noticed yet that the world wants you to be embarrassed about being a Christian? It's true—people who don't believe in Jesus will call you names and laugh at you for believing what the Bible says. They'll do everything they can to pull you away from the truth.

Jesus knew all about that. Here's the bad news: He said, "You will be hated by all people because of Me." The good news? "He who stays true to the end will be saved" (Matthew 10:22).

I am not ashamed of the Good News. It is the power of God. It is the way He saves men from the punishment of their sins if they put their trust in Him.
ROMANS 1:16

DIFFUSION

When you go to a friend's home for dinner, the first thing you might notice as you walk into the house is the smell of the food cooking. *Mmm*, smells good!

That mouthwatering smell that makes your stomach growl is an example of *diffusion*. In this case, the diffusion happens when particles of the cooking food start moving through the air until the house is filled with a great aroma.

Diffusion is the movement of particles from a place where there are a lot of particles to a place where there are fewer of them. Before long, the particles will fill both places evenly in what is called "uniform concentration." For example, if you drop a spoonful of sugar into a cup of tea, eventually the molecules of sugar will diffuse throughout the tea.

There are many examples of diffusion in nature. Your body uses diffusion when oxygen enters your lungs and then your bloodstream, and plants use diffusion when they absorb carbon dioxide and give off oxygen during photosynthesis.

The Bible doesn't use the word *diffusion*, but it gives an example of a good smell filling the air around us. When God's Spirit lives inside us, He helps us to behave in ways that please Him. And just like those food particles in the air, what we have inside us "diffuses" into the world and influences other people.

So, what can you do to make sure you're diffusing more of God's goodness?

....

We are a sweet smell of Christ that reaches up to God. It reaches out to those who are being saved from the punishment of sin and to those who are still lost in sin.
2 Corinthians 2:15

OORT CLOUD

Have you ever wondered where our solar system ends? Well, scientists believe that at the very edge of our solar system is an enormous bubble-shaped area called the *Oort Cloud*.

The Oort Cloud, which surrounds our entire solar system, is filled with billions, maybe trillions, of icy pieces of space debris—some as big as mountains on earth. Those pieces of ice and rock slowly orbit the sun, just like Earth does.

The Oort Cloud gets its name from a Dutch astronomer, Jan Oort. Back in 1950, he proposed the idea of this region to explain where some comets come from.

Scientists believe that the Oort Cloud is between 5,000 and 100,000 astronomical units from our sun. What does that mean?

Well, one astronomical unit is the distance between the earth and the sun—about 93 million miles.

Now here's a really amazing fact about the Oort Cloud: Even though scientists are convinced that it's out there, they have *no proof* of its existence. No one has ever seen it!

Does it seem odd to you that scientists are convinced something exists, even though no one has actually seen it? Well, that's a good example of faith, as Hebrews 11:1 says: "it is being sure of what we cannot see."

The Bible tells us that no one has ever seen God, yet we Christians know He exists. We see the universe and believe that there must be a Creator. We read the Bible and recognize God as the author. And we come to know Jesus, the God-man who died to save us from our sins. Right now, it's all by faith. One day, we'll see Him face-to-face!

Jesus said to him, "Thomas, because you have seen Me, you believe. Those are happy who have never seen Me and yet believe!"
JOHN 20:29

HORSEPOWER

Way back in the late 1700s, a Scottish inventor named James Watt improved a device that already existed: the steam engine. But Watt was a businessman as well as an inventor. He realized he had to figure out how to persuade miners to use his steam engine instead of horses. So Watt created a mathematical equation to compare the amount of work one steam engine could do to how many horses it would take to do the same work.

And that's how we got the term *horsepower*!

The term is now used to describe the power output of piston engines (such as internal combustion engines, like the ones in most modern cars), turbines, electric motors, and other machinery. Put simply, horsepower measures the rate at which work is done. In the United States, horsepower is measured in watts. (Can you guess why we call them watts? Yep, they were named after James Watt himself.)

Isn't it amazing that such an important scientific term as horsepower originated because a guy wanted to sell some steam engines? What a reminder that the words we use can influence the world in big ways—ways we might never imagine! That's why the Bible tells us to be careful how we talk. We should always avoid saying bad things, whether *to* other people or *about* them.

Your words have real power. Make sure you use them to help others.

Watch your talk! No bad words should be coming from your mouth. Say what is good. Your words should help others grow as Christians.
EPHESIANS 4:29

SERVOS

If you've ridden in a late-model car or an airplane, played with a toy robot, or loaded a DVD or Blu-ray to watch a movie, then you've benefited from amazing devices called servomotors (*servos* for short).

Servos are electrical devices that rotate or push other parts of a machine very accurately. Servos work well because they are small and durable. They also have built-in controls and good power for their size.

Ready for an example? In cars equipped with servos, the gas pedal sends an electronic signal that tells a car's computer how far down the pedal was pressed. The computer processes that information and sends a signal to the servo, which is attached to the car's throttle. The servo then adjusts the engine's speed.

Servos play important roles in many operations. But for the most part they are hidden from sight. You might say that servos do their work "behind the scenes."

Have you ever felt like God isn't doing anything in your life—even though you've prayed and prayed for something? Remember that God, like those servo motors, often works behind the scenes. He is way more dependable than the best servo, so you can always trust Him to look out for you—even when you can't see what He's doing or how He's doing it.

....

Jesus said to them, "My Father is still working all the time so I am working also."
JOHN 5:17

THERMAL EXPANSION

Heat has a big effect on matter—the physical stuff in our world, like the air that fills your lungs, the juice you drank at breakfast, and the chair you're sitting in right now.

In physics, the term *thermal expansion* is used to describe how matter changes in volume because of changes in temperature. Most matter tends to expand when heated, because heat causes a material's molecules or particles to start moving around and separating from one another.

Now think for a minute about the three main states of matter—solid, liquid, and gas. Out of those three, solids expand the least when they are heated. Liquids tend to expand more when heated. As you might have guessed, gases expand the most.

In the Bible, shortly after Jesus ascended to heaven, the church went through a huge expansion—not from heat, but from the energy of God's Holy Spirit. He brought together huge numbers of new Christians to grow the church from the original group of disciples into the worldwide force it is today. That growth happened as people heard the gospel—the good news of Jesus Christ—from Christians and put their faith in Jesus too.

The Holy Spirit is still helping us tell people about God. And each time we share God's story, the Lord may expand His church even more!

They gave thanks to God and all the people respected them. The Lord added to the group each day those who were being saved from the punishment of sin.
ACTS 2:47

LIQUEFACTION

In October 2018, an earthquake in Palu, Indonesia, caused many buildings to collapse. Seismologists—scientists who study earthquakes—said that the destruction occurred because of a phenomenon called earthquake *liquefaction*.

Earthquake liquefaction—also called soil liquefaction—happens when a strong quake shakes soil that is sandy, wet, and weak. The soil then starts acting very much like liquid, moving quickly downhill and often causing terrible damage. Liquefaction can damage the foundations and supports of buildings, bridges, pipelines, and roads, causing them to sink into the ground, collapse, or dissolve.

This idea from seismology might remind us of a story Jesus once told. Do you remember the time He described a wise man who had built his house on good, solid rock? Rain, floods, and wind could not make the house fall down, because its foundation was firm. But another man built his house on sand. And when the storms came, the house fell down flat!

Jesus wanted His followers to follow the first man's example and build their lives on a solid foundation. What foundation is that? The foundation of His words—and not only hearing them, but doing them. When we live in obedience to God, *nothing* can make us fall. Our lives are held up by God's almighty hands!

....

> *"Whoever hears these words of Mine and does them, will be like a wise man who built his house on rock. The rain came down. The water came up. The wind blew and hit the house. The house did not fall because it was built on rock."*
> MATTHEW 7:24–25

QRIO

What makes a good friend? Someone you can talk to is a good start. Someone who enjoys the same things you do is a plus. And a good friend always supports you in good times and bad.

Back in 2006, the electronics company Sony marketed a "robot friend" called *QRIO* (pronounced "curio"). Sony's slogan for QRIO was "To live with you, make life fun and make you happy." QRIO could walk on two legs, talk, run, dance, and even recognize a person's face and voice!

QRIO sounds pretty cool, doesn't it? But if you had one, would you really think of it as a friend? Or would you see it as an advanced gadget that *acts* like a friend only because it's programmed to do that?

The Bible tells us that God made people "in His image." That means a lot of things, but more than anything, it means that we have the ability to love God and other people. . .and we can love them *because we want to*. QRIO goes through the motions of being a friend. But it can't be a true friend because true friends, including God, choose to love you.

Do you have friends like that? If so, tell them and God how grateful you are. But if you need some true friends, ask God to help you find them. And start *being* that kind of friend too!

A man who has friends must be a friend, but there is a friend who stays nearer than a brother.
PROVERBS 18:24

MEAN

A lot of words sound the same but have very different meanings. Take the word *mean*. It could refer to an unhappy person who is hard to be around. But it's also a helpful word in statistics and mathematics.

The "arithmetic mean," as mathematicians and statisticians call it, is simply the average of a group of numbers. Mean is not hard to figure out—just add up the numbers in the group and then divide the result by how many numbers are in the group. For example, suppose you want to find out the mean height of the five starting players on your basketball team. To do that, you'd add up the heights of each player in inches and then divide by the number of players. Written down, it would look like this:

$$61 + 62 + 63 + 64 + 65 = 315$$
$$315 \div 5 = 63$$

So, the mean height of your team's starters is 63 inches, or 5 feet, 3 inches.

Sometimes, being the mean is okay. But when it comes to your Christian life, God doesn't want you to be average. He wants you to be the very best you can be and do the very best you can do. He wants you to do everything as if you're doing it for Him...then you'll be anything but average!

Whatever work you do, do it with all your heart. Do it for the Lord and not for men. Remember that you will get your reward from the Lord.
COLOSSIANS 3:23–24

MOLE

What is a *mole*? You're probably thinking of a burrowing animal that eats worms and bugs. And that is a kind of mole. But a mole is also a unit of measurement in chemistry. The mole allows chemists to compare two substances by the exact amount of atoms.

A mole equals 6.02×10^{23}—that's 602 followed by 21 zeroes! This number is also called Avogadro's number after the Italian scientist Amedeo Avogadro, who made the discovery. It represents the number of atoms in exactly 12 grams of carbon-12.

For any substance, a mole is always the same: 6.02×10^{23}. But atoms of different elements and compounds have different masses, so a mole of one substance won't *weigh* the same as a mole of another. For example, one mole of pure gold has the same number of particles as one mole of hydrogen, but gold atoms have much more mass than hydrogen atoms, so one mole of gold will weigh more than one mole of hydrogen.

Scoop up a mole of water sometime (that's about a teaspoon!) and think about this: God created a mind-blowingly huge universe, but He also created every one of the molecules of H_2O in that teaspoon. You can thank Him for the big things and the small things—even the things you can't see with the strongest microscope!

Christ made everything in the heavens and on the earth. He made everything that is seen and things that are not seen. He made all the powers of heaven. Everything was made by Him and for Him.
COLOSSIANS 1:16

FULCRUM

Some things are such everyday parts of our lives that we almost don't notice them. Like *fulcrums*.

If you want to see an example of a fulcrum, take a look at a pair of scissors. The fulcrum is the bolt or rivet that holds the handles and blades of the scissors in place so that you can move them back and forth and cut things. Without the fulcrum, a pair of scissors is just two handled blades that would be very hard to use. But together, the fulcrum and the handles make up a lever that allows you to cut paper. Levers are often called "simple machines."

The dictionary defines the word *fulcrum* as a point that a lever pivots on. But this word has another definition: an important person that something revolves around—like the boss of a big company...or the coach of a football team...or the point guard on your favorite basketball team...

. . .or *Jesus*.

When Jesus was on earth, He taught His disciples that they were to follow Him and depend on Him. They were to make Him the most important thing in their lives. If you're a Christian, Jesus wants you to make Him the fulcrum of your life. When you do that, He will live in you and help you be successful for Him.

....

"I am the Vine and you are the branches. Get your life from Me. Then I will live in you and you will give much fruit. You can do nothing without Me."
JOHN 15:5

NEWTON'S LAWS

By now you have a pretty good idea of how important a guy named Isaac Newton is to the world of science—especially a branch of science called physics. During his career, Newton came up with three basic scientific laws, called Newton's Three Laws of Motion.

The third law of motion is "for every action there is an equal and opposite reaction." Another way to say that? Forces come in pairs and they move in opposite directions. For example, when a cannonball shoots out of a cannon, the whole unit jumps backward. That's because the force of the ball leaving the cannon causes an opposite reaction in the cannon itself.

Did you know that the Bible has some things to say about equal and opposite reactions? In both the Old and New Testaments, we read that God doesn't want us to react to bad things people do or say by doing something equally bad. Instead, we should do the opposite—act or speak in *good* ways.

Jesus said it like this: "Love those who work against you. Do good to those who hate you. Respect and give thanks for those who try to bring bad to you. Pray for those who make it very hard for you" (Luke 6:27–28).

Wow! That's quite a challenge, isn't it? Being nice to someone who isn't nice to you . . . well, it's just not easy. But with God's help, you *can* respond to the bad with good.

Now, put that cannon away!

....

When someone does something bad to you, do not do the same thing to him. When someone talks about you, do not talk about him. Instead, pray that good will come to him.
1 PETER 3:9

JOULE

Back in the 1800s, there was a really smart English guy named James Prescott Joule. He was a physicist who studied heat and its relationship to mechanical work. He also formulated a unit of energy used to measure work. We call it a *joule*.

A joule is the energy exerted when the force of one newton is applied over one meter of distance. But what exactly does that mean? Well, here's an example: An average-sized apple weighs about one newton. If you want to lift the apple off a table, you have to apply one newton of upward force to counter its weight. If you lift the apple one meter high, you have done one joule of work. If you lift two apples one meter high, you have done two joules of work. If you lift 10 apples the same way...well, you get the picture.

You might never measure the work you

do in joules, but it's interesting that someone made it possible, isn't it?

In your daily life, you do all kinds of work—from schoolwork to chores in the house and out in the yard. The Bible tells us that work is very important and that God blesses those who work hard. So, no matter how you measure the work you do, do it to the best of your ability.

Your parents will be happy with you. . .and so will God!

For you will eat the fruit of your hands. You will be happy and it will be well with you.
PSALM 128:2

OBLATE SPHEROID

You've probably seen pictures of Earth taken from space, so you know that our planet is round. But would it surprise you to learn that the earth isn't *perfectly* round?

That famed scientist Isaac Newton didn't think the earth was perfectly round. He believed it is an *oblate spheroid*—a ball that is a little thicker at the equator and squashed down at the poles. (Think of it this way: if you took a basketball that didn't have quite enough air in it, placed it on the floor, and gently pushed down on the top, the round ball would become an oblate spheroid.)

Turns out that Newton was right—the actual distance from Earth's center to sea level is about 13 miles greater at the equator than at the poles.

Scientists say Earth is an oblate spheroid

because of something called centrifugal force. Earth's constant spinning causes the middle part of the planet to bulge out.

Just like Earth's spin causes it to be thicker at the equator, there are lots of things in life that shape us. What are some of the "forces" that influence us? The music we listen to. The movies and TV shows we watch. And the friends we hang out with. Good influences make us better. Bad influences don't.

So be careful about the forces you let into your life. Ask God to help you choose. He will shape you to be more and more like Jesus.

He who walks with wise men will be wise, but the one who walks with fools will be destroyed.
PROVERBS 13:20

CLOUD STORAGE

Do these funny names mean anything to you—iDrive, pCloud, Zoolz, Degoo, and OneDrive? They're all *cloud storage* services people use to stash their data so that they can keep it safe and access it on any internet-equipped device.

In the past—and it wasn't very long ago—when people wanted to store their data, they stored it on their computer's hard drive or they saved it on devices such as CDs, DVDs, USB drives, or floppy disks (ask your parents—or your grandparents—about those!). But that all changed with the invention of cloud storage.

Cloud storage involves storing data on hardware in a remote physical location, and it has a lot of advantages, including the safety and security of people's important computer data. If you want to make sure you never lose important files, use cloud storage!

Safety and security are among the most basic needs of human beings. And the Bible talks a lot about them. For Christians, safety and security are found in one place only: God's love.

God's love is so very great that absolutely nothing can take it away from us. His love is here to stay! What's more, God keeps all the wonderful things He's promised us safe in heaven (1 Peter 1:4).

....

For I know that nothing can keep us from the love of God. Death cannot! Life cannot! Angels cannot! Leaders cannot! Any other power cannot! Hard things now or in the future cannot! The world above or the world below cannot! Any other living thing cannot keep us away from the love of God which is ours through Christ Jesus our Lord.
ROMANS 8:38–39

OSMOSIS

You can perform many scientific experiments at home to see how things work in nature. For example, if you want to see how the biological principle called *osmosis* works, just drop dried fruit (like a prune or some raisins) in a glass of water. When you check on the fruit a few days later, you'll see that it has swelled up and become softer. That's because the fruit has absorbed water through the thin skin that covers it.

So, osmosis works like this: Molecules of a liquid move from one side of a "semipermeable membrane" to the other. (That big phrase is a fancy term for a barrier that liquid can pass through.) The molecules do this because they are trying to spread themselves equally on both sides of the membrane.

The word *osmosis* is also used to describe a way we learn things from another person or group of people. When we're around other people, we might not be aware that we're learning—but we're always "absorbing" ideas that will affect how we think and act. It's a little like our osmosis experiment where the water was absorbed into the fruit and made it look different.

Going to church and spending time with other Christians is a great way to learn about God and become more like Him. "Christian osmosis" is a good thing to pursue. But don't forget to spend time *alone* with God too, reading His Word and praying every day. Let's plan to learn about God every way we can!

Let us not stay away from church meetings. Some people are doing this all the time. Comfort each other as you see the day of His return coming near.
HEBREWS 10:25

BLOCK AND TACKLE

Why is a football term included in a book on science words? Well, this "block and tackle" is different. It has been around for a long time—since about 250 BC when the Greek scientist Archimedes invented it. So, what is it? It's a system of two or more pulleys with a rope or cable threaded between them.

The pulley part of Archimedes' invention is a simple machine that uses a grooved wheel and a rope. You can see pulleys today in flagpoles, window blinds, and cranes. The block and tackle is an amazing invention because it allows people to lift and move heavy objects with small amounts of human strength. A block and tackle always includes multiple pulleys—because the more pulleys you have, the more weight you can move. Believe it or not, with the right block and tackle setup, you can easily move several times your own body weight!

When Archimedes invented the block and tackle, he helped people do things they couldn't do by themselves. That's a lot like what God did for us when He sent His Holy Spirit to live inside us. God asks you to do many things that you could never do on your own. But with the help of the Holy Spirit, there's *nothing* you can't do for God.

Then he said to me, "This is the Word of the Lord to Zerubbabel saying, 'Not by strength nor by power, but by My Spirit,' says the Lord of All."
ZECHARIAH 4:6

ENGINEERING

What do you want to be when you grow up? If your perfect job includes using math and science to make things or solve technical problems, then you might want to become an engineer.

Engineering is a big subject, and there are many kinds of engineers. For example, chemical engineers use chemicals to develop things like fertilizer for crops and medicine for people and animals. Electrical engineers design electrical equipment, like computers and other devices. There are even engineers who work with atoms and other particles—they are called nanotechnology engineers.

Many engineering projects are very large and complicated and require different skills and knowledge to complete them. One example is a commercial airplane. That plane is a system of hundreds of thousands of important parts, so several types of engineers must work together to design and build it. They have to cooperate.

The Bible teaches that cooperation is a good thing because two people working together can accomplish more than just one person working alone. Even Jesus had a group of friends—His disciples—who traveled with Him as He did His job on earth.

So, how are you at cooperating? Are you a person who can work well with others to accomplish a task? Whatever God gives you to do, you'll do it much better with a helping hand.

Two are better than one, because they have good pay for their work. For if one of them falls, the other can help him up. But it is hard for the one who falls when there is no one to lift him up.
ECCLESIASTES 4:9–10

OHM'S LAW

Ohm's law (named for a German physicist, Georg Ohm) helps us to understand electrical circuits. It states that the electric current passing through a conductor is related to the voltage divided by the resistance.

What? Try thinking of Ohm's law as a simple mathematical formula:

$$I = V/R$$

In this formula, I = current in amps, V = voltage in volts, and R = resistance in ohms.

Still a little confused about how Ohm's law works? Then think of water flowing through a pipe. Imagine that the voltage (V) is the water pressure, the current (I) is the amount of water flowing, and the resistance (R) is the size of the pipe. More water can flow through the pipe when more pressure is applied and the pipe is bigger—in other words, when there is lower resistance.

In electrical systems, resistance is how much a device or material reduces the current flowing through. But there are other kinds of resistance in life. For Christians, we see resistance when other people disapprove of the way we try to live for God.

Living for Jesus isn't always easy. In fact, He told His followers that they would face opposition—*resistance*—from people who didn't want to hear His message. But He also told them that they should see themselves as blessed when people opposed them. Why? Because it proved that they were doing something right.

Yes! All who want to live a God-like life who belong to Christ Jesus will suffer from others.
2 Timothy 3:12

SONIC BOOM

Commercial airplanes travel fast—between 460 and 575 miles per hour—which is why they're great for traveling far in a short period of time. But compared to many military fighter jets, those airplanes are slowpokes. Many fighter jets can easily travel faster than the speed of sound through air...about 768 miles per hour!

When an aircraft moves faster than the speed of sound, it's said to be traveling at Mach 1. When it moves at twice the speed of sound, it's traveling at Mach 2. And when it moves at three times the speed of sound, it's traveling at Mach 3. You get the idea, right?

As an aircraft speeds up and is just about to reach the speed of sound, the sound waves produced by the plane can't move ahead of the aircraft. What happens next is really cool...and loud! The sound waves are forced together in a relatively small space and create a sonic boom.

The sound of a sonic boom is awesome to experience. But Christians will hear a much greater sound in the sky when Jesus returns for His people. The Bible says that event will come with a loud shout and blast on a horn. It will be incredible to hear—and even better as we begin eternity in heaven with Jesus.

In a very short time, no longer than it takes for the eye to close and open, the Christians who have died will be raised. It will happen when the last horn sounds. The dead will be raised never to die again. Then the rest of us who are alive will be changed.
1 CORINTHIANS 15:52

MORE GREAT STUFF FOR KIDS

Hey, kids, got a minute? Here's an educational book you'll actually *want* to read! It features 1,000 of the most important words and names of scripture—from Aaron, Abba, and Abomination to Zacchaeus, Zeal, and Zion—in understandable, even fun, language to help you know your Bible better.

Paperback / ISBN 978-1-63609-780-0

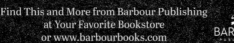